# The Byzantine Empire

*An Enthralling Overview of the Byzantium*

© Copyright 2025 - All rights reserved.

The content contained within this book may not be reproduced, duplicated, or transmitted without direct written permission from the author or the publisher.

Under no circumstances will any blame or legal responsibility be held against the publisher, or author, for any damages, reparation, or monetary loss due to the information contained within this book, either directly or indirectly.

**Legal Notice:**

This book is copyright protected. It is only for personal use. You cannot amend, distribute, sell, use, quote, or paraphrase any part, or the content within this book, without the consent of the author or publisher.

**Disclaimer Notice:**

Please note the information contained within this document is for educational and entertainment purposes only. All effort has been executed to present accurate, up-to-date, reliable, and complete information. No warranties of any kind are declared or implied. Readers acknowledge that the author is not engaging in the rendering of legal, financial, medical, or professional advice. The content within this book has been derived from various sources. Please consult a licensed professional before attempting any techniques outlined in this book.

By reading this document, the reader agrees that under no circumstances is the author responsible for any losses, direct or indirect, that are incurred as a result of the use of the information contained within this document, including, but not limited to, errors, omissions, or inaccuracies.

# Free limited time bonus

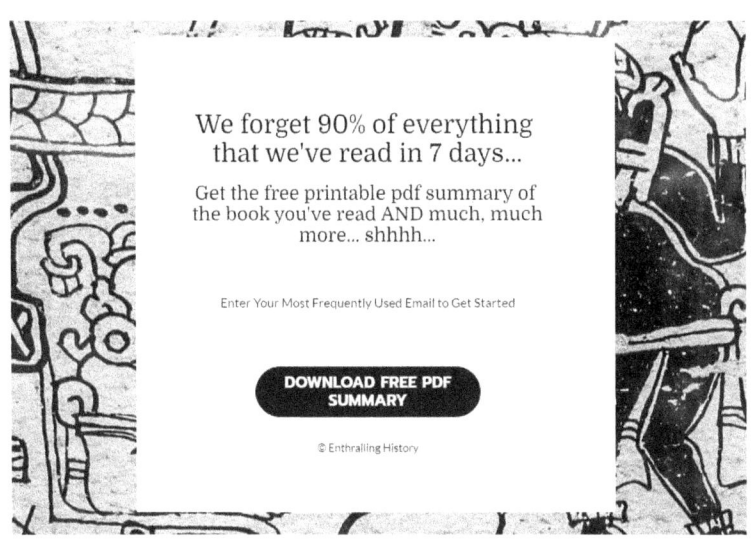

Stop for a moment. We have a free bonus set up for you. The problem is this: we forget 90% of everything that we read after 7 days. Crazy fact, right? Here's the solution: we've created a printable, 1-page pdf summary for this book that you're reading now. All you have to do to get your free pdf summary is to go to the following website: https://livetolearn.lpages.co/enthrallinghistory/

## Or, Scan the QR code!

Once you do, it will be intuitive. Enjoy, and thank you!

# Table of Contents

INTRODUCTION ................................................................................ 1
PART ONE: THE EARLY YEARS (330-565 CE) ................................ 3
    CHAPTER 1: FROM ROME TO CONSTANTINOPLE ................ 5
    CHAPTER 2: THE EMPIRE OF CHRIST ................................... 18
    CHAPTER 3: SEPARATION FROM THE WEST ........................ 28
    CHAPTER 4: JUSTINIAN'S DREAM OF RESTORATION .......... 36
PART TWO: FROM LATIN TO GREEK EMPIRES (565-867 CE) ..... 49
    CHAPTER 5: NEW ENEMIES AT THE GATES ......................... 51
    CHAPTER 6: THE ARAB INVASION .......................................... 60
    CHAPTER 7: ICONOCLASM ...................................................... 72
PART THREE: BYZANTIUM'S HEYDAY (867-1025 CE) ................ 83
    CHAPTER 8: CHRISTIANIZATION OF THE SLAVS ................ 85
    CHAPTER 9: THE BULGAR WARS ............................................ 93
    CHAPTER 10: BASIL II: THE BULGARS' DEMISE ................. 102
    CHAPTER 11: SIGNS OF DESTABILIZATION ......................... 116
    CHAPTER 12: THE GREAT SCHISM ....................................... 129
PART FOUR: DECLINE AND FALL (1081-1453 CE) ..................... 139
    CHAPTER 13: THE KOMNENIAN DYNASTY AND THE CRUSADES ................................................................................ 141
    CHAPTER 14: THE FOURTH CRUSADE AND RECOVERY ... 160
    CHAPTER 15: THE PALAIOLOGOI: THE LAST STAND ........ 170
BONUS CHAPTER: BYZANTINE ART, ARCHITECTURE, AND SOCIETY ........................................................................................ 181
CONCLUSION ............................................................................... 189
HERE'S ANOTHER BOOK BY ENTHRALLING HISTORY THAT YOU MIGHT LIKE ........................................................................ 191
FREE LIMITED TIME BONUS ...................................................... 192
REFERENCES ................................................................................ 193
IMAGE SOURCES .......................................................................... 197

# Introduction

The ultimate dissolution of the Roman Empire in 476 CE was a major event that shaped the future development of rudimentary European states. These events, occurring more than 1,500 years ago, established the fundamentals of modern-day Europe. Prior to the fall of Rome, the heritage, tradition, and power of ancient Rome moved eastward to the city of Byzantium or Constantinople, the capital of a new empire that is today known as the Byzantine Empire.

While the West was rediscovering the inventions and culture that lay in the remnants of Rome, the Byzantine Empire continued the Roman tradition. The Byzantine Empire inherited the political structure, military organization, and intellectual tradition of the old Roman Empire and started building upon these rich foundations.

The most important innovation brought on by the Byzantine Empire was, of course, the acceptance of Christianity. Constantine the Great, with his Edict of Milan, facilitated the development of a religion that took the world by storm with incredibly far-reaching consequences. It is impossible to overestimate the importance of this event. Christianity became the foundation of not only the Byzantine Empire but also of all European medieval states. It brought a major route of intellectual development in the period known, somewhat unjustified, as the "Dark Ages." The truth is that Christianity brought at least some sense of structure and hierarchy, especially in western Europe, which had been ravaged by wars and incessant barbarian invasions. It also represented a major pillar for the development of the Byzantine Empire. In turn, the Byzantine Empire allowed for the development of Christianity, with a series of councils aimed at codifying Christianity into a well-defined religious movement that could be further propagated across Europe and the world.

The Byzantine Empire managed to spread its influence across the Balkans into Russia. Serbia, Bulgaria, Romania, Montenegro, North Macedonia, Bosnia and Herzegovina (to a certain extent), Armenia, Georgia, and, last but not least, Turkey. These nations all bear marks of the Byzantine Empire, whether in terms of Orthodox Christianity, scripture, or culture. Modern-day Greece is equally proud of its ancient origins as it is proud of the days of the Byzantine Empire.

So, let's delve into the history of the Byzantine Empire, where we will discover numerous illustrious emperors, less illustrious court intrigues, and its final and inevitable decline.

# Part One:
# The Early Years
# (330–565 CE)

# Chapter 1: From Rome to Constantinople

## Prelude to Byzantium

The sheer extent of the Roman Empire in the late $3^{rd}$ and early $4^{th}$ centuries CE made effective governing of Roman lands no small feat. We must not forget that in those days, information moved at a slower pace, as did people and goods. Moreover, the Roman government was heavily centralized, which is a challenge for today's modern governments, let alone an ancient empire where it took weeks to go from one corner of the empire to the other. Even though "all roads lead to Rome," and in spite of Rome's success in Latinizing the lands it conquered, the Roman Empire was fairly diverse, with many different languages, cultures, religions, and histories.

Thus, it is not hard to understand why Emperor Diocletian, who reigned between 284 and 305 CE, decided to divide the empire. First, he divided it into two parts, himself being the head of the Eastern Empire and his chief officer, Maximian, being the head of the Western Empire. Not only that, but Diocletian (who was always the real emperor, it has to be said) formed what is now called the Tetrarchy, "the rule of the four," in 293 by appointing junior officers as co-rulers, Galerius to himself and Constantius to Maximian.

Many emperors had co-rulers. Between 161 and 169 CE, Marcus Aurelius ruled jointly with Lucius Verus as co-emperors—the first formal diarchy in Roman imperial history. In 166, Marcus appointed his son Commodus as Caesar (junior emperor), marking him as his heir.[i] Septimius Severus ruled alongside his sons, Caracalla and Geta, between 209 and 211. In a lot of cases, co-rulers, *Caesars* or *Augusti*, were mostly ceremonial, formal titles. Diocletian's Tetrarchy was more pragmatic and real. All four rulers had significant responsibilities and powers.

It seems that the most pressing demand to create the Tetrarchy was war. The Roman emperor at the time was very much the chief military commander. As war was raging in multiple corners of the empire, the most logical thing seemed to be to add more emperors who would direct the military efforts in his part of the empire. Namely, the Roman Empire faced the prospect of an "anti-emperor" elected in Britain, as well as Persian advances in the east.

It has to be stated that the Roman Empire in the late $3^{rd}$ and early $4^{th}$ centuries CE still had a very vivid memory of half a century of tumult, later called the Crisis of the Third Century (lasting from 235 to 284). As the Severus dynasty was sinking into its inevitable demise, the empire was plunging into anarchy. There was a long line of bad emperors, starting with the relatively stable Septimius Severus, who was followed by his unfortunate older son Geta, who was murdered by his brother Caracalla, a capricious emperor known for his ruthlessness and coarseness. Caracalla, in turn, was murdered by Macrinus, the head of his guard, who was himself murdered by the supporters of Elagabalus. His reign is remembered for unprecedented debauchery. The Roman Empire finally entered a period of serious decline during the reign of Severus Alexander in 235, a weak emperor who did not manage to gain obedience and respect from the military.

As can be seen, even the decades leading up to the Crisis of the Third Century were marked by instability, but the crisis itself plunged the Roman Empire into near collapse. Between 235 and 284 CE, the empire fractured into three rival entities: the Gallic Empire in the west, the central Roman Empire, and the Palmyrene Empire in the east. Over the course of this fifty-year span, approximately twenty-three emperors ruled in rapid

---

[i] Waldron, Byron Lloyd. *Diocletian, Hereditary Succession and the Tetrarchic Dynasty*. PhD diss., 2018.

succession, many of whom met violent ends.

Emperor Aurelian (r. 270-275) succeeded in reuniting the empire by defeating both the Gallic and Palmyrene breakaway states. However, despite his achievements, he was assassinated in 275 by members of his own entourage. After another decade of turmoil and six more emperors, Diocletian rose to power in 284. His ascension marked the beginning of comprehensive reforms aimed at ending the chaos and restoring stability to the Roman world.

The solution, as we have already emphasized, was obvious. The Roman Empire had to be formally divided. Besides fighting the uprising in Britain and the Persian threat, the emperors also had to deal with constant barbarian invasions in central Europe, as well as significant threats in Spain and North Africa.

Formalizing the Tetrarchy might have also been a way to ensure a smooth succession, a problem that was at the very heart of the Crisis of the Third Century.[i]

One of the tetrarchs was Constantius, surnamed Chlorus ("The White"). An able general and an experienced soldier, a necessary prerequisite for a good emperor, Constantius rose through the ranks and was declared co-ruler to Maximian around 293. A person of "great mildness, self-possession, and philosophic virtue, just, and a Neo-Platonist of the best type, a monotheist and philanthropist," Constantius was a man of great ability and power.[ii]

It is possible that he bequeathed at least some sort of enlightened spirituality to his son, Constantine. Interestingly, the times of Diocletian and his co-rulers were the last periods of Christian persecution before Constantine the Great finally granted religious freedom to Christians in 313.[iii] Although we don't really know that much about the religion of Constantine's father, we do know that Sol Invictus (Apollo) might have been Constantius's patron deity.

Diocletian established a sort of heavenly patronage system. Jupiter was the protector of Diocletian himself. Hercules was Maximian's patron,

---

[i] Ibid.

[ii] Richardson EC, Schaff P, Wace H. The life of Constantine. A Select Library of the Nicene and Post-Nicene Fathers of the Christian Church, ser. 1890;2:481-540.

[iii] Smith MD. The religion of Constantius I. Greek, Roman, and Byzantine Studies. 1997 Jun 6;38(2):187-208.

quite likely owing to the latter's physical prowess. Interestingly, a medallion that honored Constantius and his conquests in Britain bore the inscription REDDITOR LUCIS AETERNAE ("restorer of eternal light"), which was possibly a direct reference to Apollo, the deity of light. Truth be told, the parallels between the deities and tetrarchs are not clear, and scholars sometimes find variations in the deity patronage system.

Constantius, the father of Constantine the Great.[i]

There are some indications that Constantius wasn't that diligent about Diocletian's persecution of Christians. In 303, Diocletian issued an edict that ordered the closing of the churches, the forced worship of pagan gods, and the destruction of the holy Christian scriptures.[i] All Christian believers, followers, and priests were subjected to persecution. Even

---

[i] Carlan, C.U. "Life and Death in the Ancient World: The Tetrarchy and the Last Persecution of Christians (303-311)."

before this, Christian priests were ordered to make sacrifices for pagan gods, but now the whole Christian community was supposed to do it. The persecution, however, was somewhat random. In some parts of the empire, it was quite rough, but in regions governed by Maximian and Constantius Chlorus, Christians enjoyed relative peace. The two co-rulers made some symbolic gestures in favor of the edict.

It's likely that Constantius remained steeped in the pre-Christian religious landscape of the Roman Empire. An early chronicler recalls the speech of an orator at Constantius's funeral: "The temples of the gods were opened for him, and he was received by the divine conclave, and Jupiter himself extended his right hand to him."[i]

When Constantius died in 306, his son Constantine came to the forefront, the man who would revolutionize the Roman Empire and start a new empire that would last for over one thousand years. It bore the same name, but this time in Greek (Βασιλεία Ῥωμαίων), and it was, in a lot of respects, radically different than the old Roman Empire.

However, before we delve deeper into the social, economic, and political aspects of the Byzantine Empire, we will first focus on the man who made it happen: Constantine the Great.

## Constantine the Great

Born in the town of Naissus (modern-day Niš in southern Serbia), in a province where his father likely grew up, Constantine was pretty far away from the illustrious Rome. However, long gone were the days in which Roman emperors were chosen from the crème de la crème of Roman society. With the Crisis of the Third Century, it became obvious that the crown was up for grabs and that quite literally anyone could get it, provided he had enough power and ambition. Over the years, it had become a more common phenomenon for legions stationed in important provinces to declare their military leaders as emperors. This contributed to the instability of Rome; there were many provinces, many legions, and many powerful military leaders.

In the times of Diocletian, it was very much the same. Powerful legions, which drew its military strength from the local people, were stationed in the Balkan region. Diocletian was from roughly the same region as Constantine and his father (Diocletian was born in Dalmatia, modern-day

---

[i] Ibid. 194

Croatia). Maximian was from Sirmium (modern-day Sremska Mitrovica in Serbia), and Galerius was from Serdica (modern-day Sofia, capital of Bulgaria). These individuals came from provinces at the borders of the empire and had much humbler backgrounds in comparison to the typical emperors of the $1^{st}$ and $2^{nd}$ centuries CE.

Constantinus Chlorus was hailed by both the armies he led and the people in the western region of the empire. Consistent with the Roman tradition fostered in the preceding tumultuous decades, the armies greatly favored their generals and would often willingly act in the interest of their generals and against the interest of the state. In York, where Constantinus had died, Constantine was proclaimed Augustus by the armies that had been under the command of his father.

**Early Reign**

Constantine first assumed control of his father's vast territories, which included Gaul and Britain (the modern-day United Kingdom, France, and western parts of Germany). By this time, the Tetrarchy had started to devolve into the sort of chaos so characteristic of the Roman Empire. Without going into too much detail about every person involved in the civil wars of Constantine's early reign, we're going to paint the basic backdrop of the landscape of the early $4^{th}$-century city of Rome.

Although Diocletian's Tetrarchy aimed to divide imperial power and provide solid checks on the power of each emperor, internal strife was inevitable. In theory, Diocletian and Maximian held the senior imperial title of Augustus, each overseeing half of the empire. Under them were their junior colleagues, Galerius and Constantius Chlorus, who held the subordinate title of Caesar. When the time came, Diocletian and Maximian would be replaced by the two Cesares, which would ensure a smooth and peaceful succession. Both Diocletian and Maximian, miraculously for Roman emperors, abdicated in 305. The Tetrarchy wouldn't last for much longer.

A few unfortunate events made a smooth succession much more complex. First of all, Galerius didn't really want to let Constantius and Maxentius (son of Maximian and contestant for the throne) dominate the Roman Empire after the two Augusti had abdicated. Shortly after the departure of Diocletian and Maximian, Galerius promoted two people of his own choosing to the rank of Ceasar: Severus II and Maximinus Daza. The matter was made even more confusing when Constantius died and left control of Rome's northeastern regions under his son's command.

The armies under Constantine's command were too powerful and loyal for Galerius to immediately face Constantine.

Galerius's disregard for Maximian's son, Maxentius, cost him dearly. Maxentius launched an attack on Galerius in Italy in 307, defeating Severus II, who had been sent by Galerius. He assumed control of Italy and North Africa and held his positions until 312.

Constantine the Great.[1]

Meanwhile, Constantine decided to lay low, avoid the conflict in Italy, and get things sorted out in his provinces. He was popular very early on due to the people's vivid and positive memories of his father. Constantine earned a reputation for his able leadership of his provinces, focusing on infrastructure (such as building roads), stability, and peace.

The event that laid the foundation for the next millennia of the emerging Byzantine Empire came in 312. Constantine decided to conquer Rome to reunify the Roman Empire under his authority. To this end, he formed an alliance with Licinius, a former friend of Galerius, who was in

Gaul at the time. Thanks to this alliance, Licinius would become Augustus and ruler of the East.

Constantine's army of twenty-five thousand men crossed the Alps. Once they were in Italy, they took the city of Susa, defeated Maxentius's troops in Turin, and captured Milan in a series of blistering victories.

Maxentius was preparing for a final battle to preserve his reign in Rome and decided not to let Constantine lay siege to another city. Instead, he decided to face Constantine's army in an open battle, which would turn out to be a fatal error.

On October 28$^{th}$, 312, a few kilometers north of Rome on the Milvian Bridge, the two armies clashed, reshaping the history of the Roman Empire.

According to Eusebius, Constantine said that about noon, when the day was already beginning to decline, he saw a cross of light in the heavens, above the sun, bearing the inscription IN HOC SIGNO VINCES ("conquer with this sign"). It was said he was struck with amazement and that his whole army also witnessed the miracle.

"He said, moreover, that he doubted within himself what the import of this apparition could be. And while he continued to ponder and reason on its meaning, night suddenly came on; then in his sleep the Christ of God appeared to him with the same sign which he had seen in the heavens, and commanded him to make a likeness of that sign which he had seen in the heavens, and to use it as a safeguard in all engagements with his enemies."[i]

Maxentius's army has been said to be so numerous that its formation was as deep as it was wide, counting as many as thirty thousand men. Yet, the risky tactic left Maxentius's army without room for maneuver or retreat and encouraged Constantine to attack. His veteran army managed to push the cavalry toward the Milvian Bridge, at which point Maxentius and his reserve infantry tried to run across the Tiber. Some of the fleeing infantry managed to get away, but most of Maxentius's men were cut down. Maxentius himself fell onto the wooden boat bridge built prior to the battle, which got destroyed, and he was swallowed by the Tiber, ending his life.

---

[i] Hunt, E.D. *Eusebius of Caesarea, Life of Constantine*. Translated by Averil Cameron and Stuart G. Hall. *The Journal of Ecclesiastical History* 52, no. 2 (2001): 338-396.

Meanwhile, to the north, the Praetorian forces surrounded by Constantine's army made their final stand. Amazed by their courage, newly Christian-converted Constantine decided to spare their lives.

**Amassing Power**

Following this victory, Constantine claimed the entire Western Roman Empire for himself, while his ally, Licinius, claimed the Eastern Roman Empire. Constantine became the first Christian emperor of Rome.

Constantine sought to elevate his brother-in-law, Bassianus, possibly to the rank of Caesar, and entrusted him with authority in Italy. However, before the appointment could be finalized, Bassianus was implicated in a conspiracy against Constantine, allegedly at the instigation of his brother Senecio, a close ally of Licinius. When Constantine demanded that Licinius hand over Senecio for punishment, Licinius refused. This breakdown in diplomacy contributed directly to the renewal of civil war between the two emperors.

In 316, Constantine won the Battle of Cibalae despite being outnumbered. He conquered the entire Balkan Peninsula, apart from Thrace and Lower Moesia, and made Licinius agree to a peace deal. Nevertheless, in 324, the conflict resumed when Constantine's army went into Licinius's territory in pursuit of a raiding force of Visigoths, which Licinius interpreted as a direct attack on his own forces. Licinius placed his army in a two-hundred-stadia-long defensive formation in the Battle of Adrianople, but Constantine used a clever trick.[i] He sneakily crossed the river to make the enemy withdraw. Once Licinius's army took a defensive position on a higher ground, an onslaught ensued, from which Constantine emerged as the victor.[ii]

---

[i] A stadion (plural stadia) was an ancient unit for measuring length. One stadion equaled about 150 meters. The unit got its name from ancient stadiums used to host games, such as the Olympics.

[ii] Zosimus, Historia nova, English translation: R.T. Ridley, Zosimus: New History, Byzantina Australiensia 2, Canberra (1982).

Licinius.[a]

Following the defeat, Licinius retreated to Byzantium, which Constantine besieged. Constantine's son Crispus commanded the fleet in the Battle of the Hellespont, where he inflicted another defeat on Licinius's forces. Following this naval victory, Constantine the Great faced Licinius's army in the final battle of the war, Chrysopolis. After the ultimate defeat of Licinius, Constantine became the first man to rule the entirety of the Roman world since Maximian became Diocletian's co-emperor in 286.[i]

### From Byzantium to Constantinople

The city of Constantinople was built on the foundations of a much older town, Byzantium. Byzantium was founded by the polis of Megara, a mid-sized city-state between Corinth and Athens, in 657 BCE. To this day, scholars don't know for sure why it was placed on the eastern side of the Bosphorus, given that the tides are more favorable on the western side. A

---

[i] Dunstan, W.E. (2010) Rome, Rowman & Littlefield Publishers, Lanham MD. ISBN 9780742568341

common explanation is that unfavorable tides made it harder for enemies to approach by sea, and if Byzantium was attacked by land, the enemy army would be forced into a narrow strip, giving Byzantium a unique military advantage.

The city saw a period of expansion during the reign of Emperor Septimius Severus, who ruled between 193 and 211. New sets of defensive walls were built, as well as other great structures, such as the Baths of Zeuxippus and the Hippodrome. These structures were Severus's most important and enduring legacy. Following the victory over his rivals in 324, Constantine renamed Byzantium, firstly to New Rome and later to Constantinople, making it his new capital.

Map of Constantinople.[4]

By Constantine's time, the center of power had shifted to the east, where three-quarters of the Roman population and wealth were located, making relocation of the capital a politically viable move. A factor that also played a great role was that Constantine, even though he was the son of an emperor, did not come from an aristocratic Roman family. He was looked down upon by Roman aristocrats. By being the sole ruler in Byzantium, his own city, he would ensure the stability of power far away from the intrigues of Rome.

Constantine's first step in making Constantinople was the construction of the Walls of Constantinople, outgrowing the city's former boundary. Even though they were outdated by 420, and the city continued to add new fortifications, some parts of the Walls of Constantinople can still be seen in modern-day Istanbul.

Constantine also enhanced and decorated the Baths of Zeuxippus with around eighty statues of numerous historical figures, such as Homer and Demosthenes, along with various heroes and gods. The fact that pagan deities stood in the middle of the newly founded city of Constantinople debunks the myth that Constantine's intention was to create an entirely Christian city.
The Hippodrome, another construction rebuilt by Constantine, remained one of the key centers until the fall of the Byzantine Empire. It was a place where the emperor could observe the people and allow them to let off steam. It was also a place where great tumult and revolts, such as the Nika riots, would take place.

Once the Hippodrome was renovated, it was about 450 meters long and 130 meters wide, capable of holding 100,000 spectators. The Kathisma (the emperor's lodge) was accessible directly from the Great Palace of Constantinople through a passage only the emperor and other members of the imperial family could use.

Constantine relocated important monuments from the Mediterranean and placed them at the center of the Hippodrome, including the Obelisk of Thutmose III (erected during the Eighteenth Dynasty by Pharaoh Thutmose III (r. 1479–1425 BCE)) and the Serpent Column (made to celebrate Greece's victory over Mardonius and the Persians in the Battle of Plataea in 479 BCE).

Emperor Constantine the Great dedicated Constantinople on May 11th, 330, by performing a bloodless sacrifice. He honored the city's deity, Tyche, and some traditions suggest he named her Anthousa. However, he also placed the city under the protection of the Virgin Mary, marking its Christian foundation.

Constantine the Great built a statue of himself, holding the protector of the city, Anthousa (Tyche), in his right hand. Constantine ordered that on the day of the races held in honor of the city's founding, his statue should be brought into the Hippodrome accompanied by soldiers dressed in cloaks and campagi (ceremonial lace-up boots traditionally worn by emperors, consuls, and high-ranking officials) while carrying candles. The statue was placed on a cart and taken around the track in a ceremonial circuit before being brought to a stand opposite the imperial box. At this point, the reigning emperor would rise, face the statue of Constantine—alongside the city's divine protector—and bow in a gesture of reverence.[1]

By far the most important and most fascinating building in Constantinople was Hagia Sophia, the temple of the empire's new religion, Christianity. Initially, the city must have looked fairly similar to ancient Roman or Greek cities, with the Hippodrome dominating the landscape. However, Constantinople and numerous other cities in the Byzantine Empire would oversee the construction of an entirely new category of buildings: early Christian temples.

In the next chapter, we'll address the roots of Christianity and how it managed to take over the Byzantine Empire.

---

[1] Jeffreys, Elizabeth. "The Beginning of Byzantine Chronography: John Malalas." In *Greek and Roman Historiography in Late Antiquity*. Brill, 2003. pp. 497–527.

# Chapter 2: The Empire of Christ

## Early Christianity: Not the Christianity We Know Today

The Byzantine Empire's development was influenced by the organization of the Roman state, Greek culture, and the Christian faith. That merging happened as a consequence of the decentralization and decline of the Roman Empire due to the Crisis of the Third Century. As mentioned before, the Crisis of the Third Century left the empire in a state of chaos. But from this chaos emerged a sort of structure, a blend of Greco-Roman culture and Christianity, which provided fertile ground for the development of a new European powerhouse fueled by the growth of the Orthodox Church.

To truly understand the origins of Christianity, we must first briefly delve into some predecessor currents of religious thought.

## Origins of Christianity

During the Bronze Age, in the regions of ancient Israel and Judah, the religion of the Israelites (Yahwism, as scholars today call it) arose.[i] It was initially polytheistic. Yahweh and his consort, Asherah, were seen as superior to the second-tier divinities, such as Baal, Shamash, Astarte, Yarikh, and Mot. All these gods and goddesses had their own priests,

---

[i] Miller, Patrick D. (2000). The Religion of Ancient Israel. Westminster John Knox Press. ISBN 978-0-664-22145-4.

prophets, and royalty among their devotees.[i] Priests of the time largely advocated for henotheism, calling for adherence to one particular god, Yahweh, while still recognizing other gods. The Temple in Jerusalem was the most significant place of worship to the Israelite king, who was seen as God's worldly governor.

The Kingdom of Israel fell to the Assyrians, and the nearby Kingdom of Judah and its capital, Jerusalem, managed to keep the Israelite religion alive, with the Temple of HaShem (meaning "the name," Yahweh) as its center. Once the Kingdom of Judah was conquered by the Babylonians, the Temple was destroyed, and Judah's elites were carried off to Babylon, an occurrence we now remember as the Babylonian Exile, which lasted from 586 to 516 BCE. From that point in time, the Israelites became known as Jews, named after the fallen kingdom.

The Persians who had conquered the Babylonians allowed the Jews to return to Jerusalem and rebuild the Temple, thus marking the era of the Second Temple, which lasted from 516 BCE to 70 CE. The importance of this cannot be understated, as the original Israelite religion became highly influenced by Persian philosophy. The religion of the Persian Empire at the time was Zoroastrianism, one of the oldest monotheistic religions, which largely influenced the belief systems of Judaism, Christianity, and Islam. It is most likely that the concept of Satan and the divine battle between good and evil, in which good will emerge victorious, came from this ancient Persian religion. Zoroastrianism is still practiced to this day, with about 120,000 followers worldwide.

Four sects of Judaism existed at the time, one of which became the foundation of Judaism as it exists today. The Sadducees were active in Judea during the Second Temple period up until its destruction in 70 CE. They were associated with the elites of Judean society, and their priests ran the Temple since they were the most open to Hellenistic influences.[ii]

The Pharisees, on the other hand, were associated with the common man. Its scholars studied Hebrew scriptures. They emerged around 150 BCE and resisted Hellenistic influence. While the Sadducees emphasized the importance of the Temple and its rituals, the Pharisees focused on

---

[i] Handy, Lowell K. (1995). "The Appearance of Pantheon in Judah". In Edelman, Diana Vikander (ed.). The Triumph of Elohim: From Yahwism to Judaism. Peeters Publishers. ISBN 90-5356-503-5.

[ii] "The Antiquities of the Jews (13.298)".

Mosaic law and oral tradition. After the Romans destroyed the Second Temple in 70 CE, the Sadducees lost their influence, while the Pharisees' adaptable model of worship and law interpretation survived. Many Jews were killed or enslaved during the siege, but Pharisaic teachers regrouped in other regions, eventually evolving into the rabbinic leadership that shaped what is now known as Rabbinic Judaism—the foundation of modern Jewish practice.

The Essenes were the sect known to be the most mystical. They usually lived apart from mainstream society and had a keen interest in angels and the spiritual Messiah, seeing themselves as the genuine remnants of Israel who upheld the true covenant with God. Scholars believe that the Dead Sea Scrolls are the library of the Essenes. In contrast to the Essenes, the Zealots worked toward real-world change, namely the political freedom of Jews and the overthrow of the Roman government.

### Early Christianity

The fifth Jewish sect is Christians. A large number of Christian denominations have come about and perished over the centuries. The term "early Christianity" refers to the period between Jesus' death and the Council of Nicaea in 325 CE.

Early on, in the 1st century CE, almost all Christians were Jews. Apostle Paul, a former Pharisee, was the one responsible for attracting the Gentiles (God-fearing non-Jews) who were somewhat sympathetic toward Judaism but were not Hebrews. (Gentiles could not convert to Judaism, mostly due to the fact that Judaism, especially at the time, was closely related to the Hebrew ethnicity, so one could rarely convert to Judaism if they had not been born as a Hebrew Jew.)

Many early Christians were merchants who created churches (in that time, the term was taken in its literal sense, ἐκκλησία, meaning "gathering" or "congregation"). More accurately, they held services in small private homes.[i] More than forty Christian communities existed in cities around the Mediterranean by the end of the 1st century, laying the foundation for its expansion.[ii]

---

[i] Liddell, Henry George, and Robert Scott. *A Greek-English Lexicon*. The Perseus Project.

[ii] Hitchcock, Susan Tyler, and John L. Esposito. *Geography of Religion: Where God Lives, Where Pilgrims Walk*. National Geographic Society, 2004. p. 281.

Early Christianity was very much influenced by Judaism, but it also influenced the Jewish community in a major way. Numerous Jews converted to Christianity. While the Zealots were primarily a political-religious movement that opposed Roman occupation, it is possible that some individuals with Zealot sympathies later embraced Christianity. One of the apostles, Simon the Zealot—also referred to as Simon the Canaanite—is traditionally believed to have had such associations, although the exact meaning of his title remains debated. Some scholars have also noted the influence of the Essenes on early Christianity. Their emphasis on divine revelation, dualism, and the coming of a messianic age bears resemblance to certain early Christian themes.[i]

Before we delve into the Council of Nicaea, it is important to know that it was not the first Christian council. A common misconception people often hold is that Christianity was a free-for-all in terms of interpretation of the scripture. For example, a number of post-apostolic councils were held in Rome and elsewhere sometime in the $2^{nd}$ and $3^{rd}$ centuries. The problem that emerged during the mid-$2^{nd}$ century was the rise of Montanism, a belief system that stated the Trinity consisted of only a single person, meaning that Christ's humanity was absorbed by his divinity. This sect was also more radical, discipline-wise. For instance, according to Montanism, once a Christian fell out of grace, they could not be redeemed. Their restoration to the church would be impossible.

During that time, many other belief systems that were associated with Christianity were influential. Gnosticism was one of them. Gnosticism was not a single, unified belief system but rather a collection of diverse teachings and sects that are grouped under the umbrella term "Gnostic." They believed that the physical world was imperfect and evil and that through knowledge (*gnosis* means "wisdom"), they could access the perfect spiritual world. They downplayed Jesus' humanity, placing emphasis on his divinity. Yet, some sources describe Yahweh as being a malevolent lesser deity who created this vile world.[ii] Even though early church fathers condemned Gnosticism as heresy, its schools of thought were very influential. More orthodox Christians did their best to destroy

---

[i] Hamidovic, David. "About the Links Between the Dead Sea Scrolls and Mandaean Liturgy." *Aram Periodical* 22 (2010): 441-451.

[ii] Pagels, Elaine. The Gnostic Gospels. Knopf Doubleday. (1989) ISBN 978-0-679-72453-7.

the Gnostic scriptures, a task in which they were almost fully successful.[i]

Valentinianism and Sethianism, two distinct Gnostic teachings, spread across the Persian Empire, and a related movement called Manichaeism spread all the way to China. To this day, there is a Gnostic religion in modern-day Iraq called Mandaeism (sometimes referred to as Sabianism or Nasoraeanism) that considers Adam (the first human, according to the Bible) to be the founder of the religion and John the Baptist its greatest prophet. Jesus is considered to be a false prophet.[ii] Its adherents today range somewhere between sixty thousand and one hundred thousand. [iii] They manage to keep their belief system alive even though they suffer oppression.

To illustrate early divisions in Christian theology, let's look at Marcionism, a movement founded by Marcion of Sinope around 144 CE in Rome. Marcion, the son of a bishop from Pontus (modern-day Turkey), was influenced by dualistic and Gnostic ideas. He rejected the Hebrew Scriptures (the Old Testament), viewing the God described there—the creator of the material world—as a lower, imperfect deity known as the Demiurge. He believed the God revealed in the New Testament was the true, supreme, and benevolent deity.[iv]

Marcion dismissed many Christian writings that did not align with this view and compiled his own version of the Christian canon, including a heavily edited Gospel of Luke and ten of Paul's epistles. He considered the Apostle Paul the only true apostle who correctly understood Jesus' message.[v] Although Marcion's teachings were declared heretical by the early church, they sparked significant debates and influenced the early development of Christian doctrine and the biblical canon

---

[i] Layton, Bentley. "Prolegomena to the study of ancient Gnosticism". In White, L. Michael; Yarbrough, O. Larry (eds.). (1995) The Social World of the First Christians: Essays in Honor of Wayne A. Meeks. Minneapolis: Fortress Press. ISBN 978-0-8006-2585-6.
[ii] Edmondo, Lupieri. "Friar of Ignatius of Jesus (Carlo Leonelli) and the First 'Scholarly' Book on Mandaeism (1652)." *ARAM Periodical* 16 (2004): 25–46.
[iii] Thaler, Kai. "Iraqi Minority Group Needs U.S. Attention." *Yale Daily News*, 9 March 2007. Retrieved 4 November 2021.
[iv] Ehrman, Bart D. *Lost Christianities: The Battles for Scripture and the Faiths We Never Knew.* Oxford: Oxford University Press, 2005. pp. 95–112. ISBN 978-0-19-518249-1.
[v] Ibid.

Just how powerful these non-orthodox teachings were can be seen in the fact that Augustine of Hippo, who lived in the 4th and 5th centuries CE and was born decades after the Nicene Creed was created, was, for a long time, a Manichean. He became a Manichean after arriving in Rome.

The landscape of Christianity was incredibly diverse, and while there were more or less orthodox currents, centuries would have to pass before the establishment of an institution that could be referred to as an official church in the modern sense.

### Establishment of the Official Faith

While there are many events that shaped Christianity as we know it today, two major decisions made by Constantine are arguably the most important.

In February 313, via the Edict of Milan, Emperor Constantine, together with Licinius, granted Christianity legal status in the Roman Empire, ending centuries of persecution of Christians and paving the way for the Christian faith to become the foundation of the Western world we know today.[i] This did not mean that Christianity became the official faith of the Roman Empire; it only meant that Christians were now allowed to worship freely and without fear of persecution.

Some historians argue that this edict shouldn't be seen as an act of genuine faith on Constantine's part; instead, it should be seen as a pragmatic political decision. Constantine considered the Christian god to be such a strong and influential deity that an alliance had to be made to ensure the stability of the empire and avoid his wrath.[ii] Nevertheless, it is more probable that it was an act of true faith since Constantine's favors to Christianity in his lifetime were many.[iii]

This leads us to the Council of Nicaea. There is a common misconception regarding the first ecumenical council that needs to be addressed. It is often mentioned that in Nicaea, bishops agreed upon which scriptures would become part of the canon and which ones would be discarded. The most important bishops gathered in Nicaea because there was a big crisis within the Christian faith, and this crisis threatened to divide Christianity.

---

[i] The Cambridge History of Christianity - Cambridge University Press.
[ii] Sordi, Marta. *The Christians and the Roman Empire.* Norman: University of Oklahoma Press, 1994. p. 134.
[iii] Maier, Paul L. *Eusebius: The Church History.* Grand Rapids: Kegel Publications, 1999. p. 374.

A later icon depicting the Nicene Creed.[5]

The problematic teaching was a heresy called Arianism, named after Bishop Arius of Alexandria. In his attempt to defend the oneness of God, he separated the Father (a transcendental being not confined by the universe) from the Holy Spirit and the Son, Jesus Christ. He referred to Christ as *homoiousios* (a term coined in Greek, with *homoios* meaning "similar" and *ousia* meaning "essence"). This means he thought that Christ the Son was subordinate to God, which diminished his divinity.

To resolve this division, Constantine called for an ecumenical council (a council of all the church's bishops) to ensure religious stability. Constantine's personal involvement in Christian affairs set a precedent that many kings and emperors would follow. He convened an ecumenical council in Nicaea and summoned all 1,800 bishops of the known Christian world.

The debate raged for sixty-six days, from May 20^th to July 25^th, 325.[i] Out of 381 bishops that were present near Constantine's summer palace, the loudest proponents of opposing views were Arius of Alexandria, after whom Arianism was named, and Athanasius of Alexandria, whom Christians came to worship as a saint both by the Eastern Orthodox Church and the Catholic Church.[ii, iii] The debate was fierce, and upon being cleverly questioned, Arius admitted that Christ is a created creature, which implies he is a limited being and that his death for humanity's sins couldn't have redeemed us. That meant both Christ and the Holy Spirit were separate from the Father, bringing polytheism back into the game. According to Damaskinos, an Athenian monk, Saint Nicholas of Myra, at one point stood in front of Arius and slapped him in front of all of the church fathers and Constantine, who was present for the entirety of the council.[iv]

By the end of the sixty-six-day council, the Nicene Creed was agreed upon. Christ was to be referred to as *homoousion,* the same in being and the same in essence as the Father. Those who "assert that the Son of God is of different hypostasis or substance, or created, or is subject to alteration or change" would be looked down on.[v] Furthermore, Constantine issued an edict that Arius's writings were to be burned to erase his teachings, going as far as to command "that if someone should be discovered to have hidden a writing composed by Arius, and not have immediately brought it forward and destroyed it by fire, his penalty shall be death."[vi]

Yet, the story of Arianism lived on until the 7^th century. Following the establishment of Nicene Christianity, there were issues with Athanasius. He was accused of murder, sorcery, and treason. The First Synod in Tyre was convened in 335 to address these allegations, and Athanasius was excommunicated. This synod, interestingly, also saw Arius be absolved of his wrongdoings.[vii] Constantine himself was baptized by Eusebius of

---

[i] Wheeler, Joe L. *Saint Nicholas*. Thomas Nelson, 2010.
[ii] Theodoret of Cyrus, The Ecclesiastical History of Theodoret, Book 3, Chapter 31
[iii] "Online Chapel - Greek Orthodox Archdiocese of America". *www.goarch.org*
[iv] Wheeler, Joe L. *Saint Nicholas*. Thomas Nelson, 2010.
[v] The Nicene Creed, which was agreed to at the council in 325.
[vi] "Emperor Constantine's Edict against the Arians." *fourthcentury.com*. 23 January 2010. Archived from the original on 19 August 2011. Retrieved 20 August 2011.
[vii] Socrates of Constantinople. *Church History*, Book 1, Chapter 33. In Anthony F. Beavers, *Chronology of the Arian Controversy.*

Nicomedia, a priest sympathetic to Arius, on his deathbed.[i] His son, Constantinus II, who inherited the throne, was also somewhat sympathetic to Arianism. Constantine's grandson Julian was the only emperor of the Byzantine Empire who rejected Christianity, seeing himself as a pure "Hellene."

Even though Julian's successor, Jovian, was a Christian, he only reigned for eight months, never even entering Constantinople. That's when Valens, an Arian, became the ruler of the empire for fourteen years, from 364 to 378. Having an Arian emperor for nearly fifteen years led to the restoration of lost rights for Arians. This continued the debate and the somewhat precarious status of Christianity within the Byzantine Empire throughout the rest of the 4th century.

It was not until Theodosius I, a devout Nicene Christian, that Christianity finally became the official religion of the empire. The Edict of Thessalonica was issued on February 27th, 380 CE, by Emperor Theodosius I of the Eastern Roman Empire and the Western co-emperors Gratian and the young Valentinian II.[ii]

Theodosius I.[a]

Theodosius I was able to restore political stability in the East, which allowed the Goths to settle in Roman territory. With his increasing power, he defeated the usurpers Magnus Maximus and Eugenius. In 381, he convened the second ecumenical council, known as the First Council of Constantinople, which condemned paganism and established Nicene Christianity over Arianism. He was the last emperor to hold power over both the Eastern and Western parts of the empire.

---

[i] Gonzalez, Justo. *The Story of Christianity*, Vol. 1. Harper Collins, 1984. p. 176. ISBN 0-06-063315-8.
[ii] Ehler, Sidney Zdeneck; Morrall, John B (1967). *Church and State Through the Centuries: A Collection of Historic Documents with Commentaries*

Arcadius took the throne in the East, while the Western soldier-emperors were under the rule of his son Honorius. After the death of Arcadius, his heir, Theodosius II, entrusted a loyal ally, Anthemius, and other officials with the task of building the Theodosian Walls to defend Constantinople. Since he had others deal with the matters of the capital, his focus shifted toward theological disputes and the formulation of the *Codex Theodosianus*. The codex aimed to clear up confusion and establish a single code of law, reinforcing Christianity as the empire's official religion. It contained some of the first laws granting tax exemptions to the church, which were originally passed by Constantine and Constantius II. In 431, Emperor Theodosius II convened the third ecumenical council, the Council of Ephesus, to address the teachings of Nestorius, who believed that Jesus had two separate persons, human and divine. The council condemned Nestorianism and affirmed Mary's title as Theotokos, or "mother of God."[1]

Eutyches, in contrast to Nestorius, denied the humanity of Christ and held a Monophysite view of Christ's nature. The Second Council of Ephesus in 449, called by Theodosius II toward the end of his rule, addressed this new view. It was one of the most controversial councils of the time. However, the decisions made at this council were ultimately rejected by the wider Christian community, leading to further divisions in the church.

Theodosius's successor, Marcian, almost immediately convened another council in 451, the Council of Chalcedon. This council affirmed the Chalcedonian definition that declared Christ to be perfect in godhood and manhood. Eutyches's Monophysitism was rejected, marking a significant turning point in theological debates.

Although there were sporadic and short-lived returns to paganism, such as with Emperor Julian, the Eastern Roman Empire was strongly defined by Christianity.

---

[1] Ostrogorsky, George, *History of the Byzantine state*, Rutgers University Press, 1969, p.78

# Chapter 3: Separation from the West

## Wars with Germanic Tribes, the Invasion of the Huns, and the Battle of Adrianople

The Western Roman Empire was heading toward its complete demise due to ongoing internal instability, economic challenges, and barbarian invasion. In 375, the nomadic confederation known as the Huns breached Europe through the passage between the Caspian Sea and the Ural Mountains, sometimes colloquially referred to as "the gate (or passage) of the peoples."[i] The Roman Empire faced numerous battles along its northern and western borders, but most of the power was situated in the Eastern Roman Empire. It was up to the Eastern emperor to fight on two fronts.

---

[i] It seems there is no definitive translation of this term, but it is frequently used in many Slavic languages.

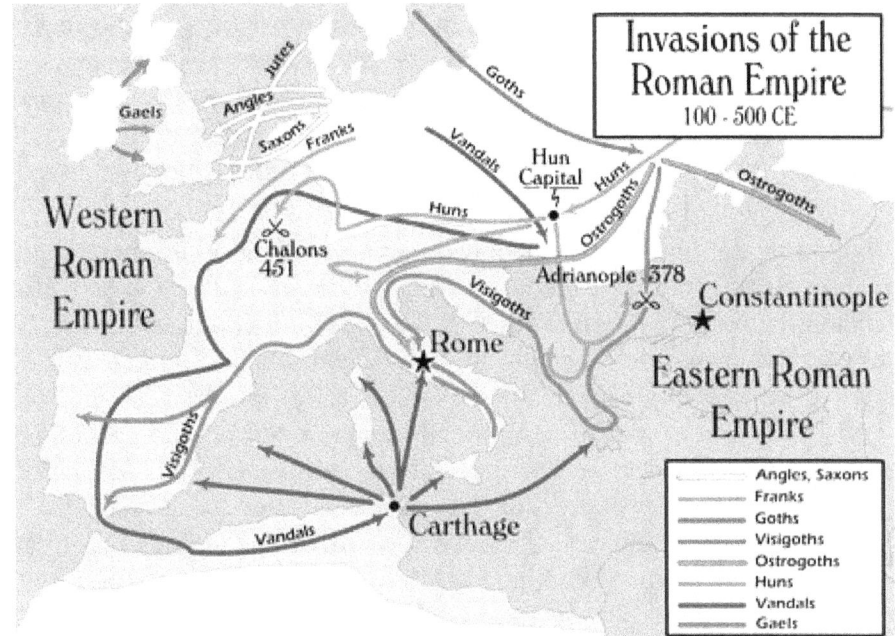

Map depicting the invasions of the Roman Empire.⁷

Valens (r. 364-378), who ruled in the East, was the first emperor to face this two-front war. He aided his brother, Valentinian II, in the western provinces while simultaneously defending the Eastern Empire from Persian attacks.

An Eastern Germanic tribe, the Goths, played a significant role in the decline of the Western Roman Empire. They fled from the advancing Hun army, which left devastation in its wake, and the Goths sought refuge in the Roman Empire. They arrived in Roman territory in 376.[i] However, they were mistreated by Roman officials, leading to a revolt. One of the most significant outcomes of the Hun threat was the Goths' sack of Adrianople in 378. Emperor Valens, who had been dealing with the Persian army on the eastern front, moved to the Balkan Peninsula.

Ignoring pleas from his nephew Gracian, Valentinian's successor, Valens insisted on confronting the enemy alone. He underestimated the size and strength of the Gothic forces, and he and his army were defeated after the Goths pillaged Thrace.[ii] This event marked a significant shift in the perception of Roman invincibility. It emboldened other tribes to

---

[i] Painter, Sidney, *A History of the Middle Ages 284-1500*, The MacMillan Press LTD, 1973, p.33
[ii] Ostrogorsky, George, *History of the Byzantine State,* Rutgers University Press, 1969, p.72

challenge Roman authority and led to increased instability in the region. The attack highlighted the vulnerability of Roman military tactics to nomadic cavalry-based armies. This demonstration of cavalry supremacy served as a model for future wars.[i] Even though the Huns did not directly participate in the battle, their presence compelled other tribes to engage in action, strengthening the influence of the Huns in Europe.

Following the Hunnic invasion, two major Gothic groups emerged: the Visigoths in the west and the Ostrogoths in the east. The Gothic Wars predated the reign of Theodosius I (r. 379-395) but continued during his rule after he took over the throne after Valens died. Seeking to quell further unrest, Theodosius dealt with Gothic tribes, primarily suppressing the Visigoths and Ostrogoths. Although he attempted peace negotiations, he ultimately decided to engage in a military campaign in Thrace in 380, which was not entirely successful. Nevertheless, Theodosius managed to conclude a peace treaty with Visigothic King Athanaric in 382. This treaty was a significant moment in Roman-Gothic relations and set a precedent for future agreements, allowing the Goths to settle within the empire and maintain autonomy on their land in return for military service and loyalty.

## Wars with Sasanian Persians

On the eastern border, the Eastern Roman Empire and the Sasanian Persian Empire were involved in several wars and other minor conflicts during the $4^{th}$ century. Although the conflict predated and lasted after the $4^{th}$ century, some of the longest and most significant wars between the two empires took place during this century. It started during the reign of Constantine the Great (r. 306-337) and continued into the reign of Emperor Julian the Apostate (r. 361-363), and it involved multiple campaigns and battles. After King Shapur II (309-379) regained control of the territory that is now Afghanistan and Pakistan, he launched a campaign against the Romans in 359.[ii] In response, Emperor Julian launched a major campaign spanning the next four years, culminating in the Battle of Ctesiphon in 363, where Emperor Julian was killed.

The conflict ended with his successor, Jovian, signing a treaty that returned the territories the Romans had taken from the Sasanian Empire. During the reign of Theodosius I, relatively peaceful relations were

---

[i] Bury, J.B. *The Invasion of Europe by the Barbarians*, W.W. Norton & Company, 2000, p.42

[ii] Shapur II acquired the title at birth and held it until his death at age seventy, making him the longest-reigning monarch in Iranian history.

maintained with the Sasanian Empire, partly due to internal challenges and threats from other powers. However, conflicts arose as Theodosius I solidified the power of the Eastern Empire. Disputes over the division of Armenia between the Romans and Sasanians sparked this conflict. Both empires wanted to exert their influence, and in 387, a major revolt erupted in Armenia against Sasanian rule. The rebels sought assistance from the Eastern Roman Empire, leading to increased tensions. Under King Shapur III, the son of Shapur II, the Sasanians invaded Roman territories in Armenia and Mesopotamia. The war ended with the signing of the Treaty of Acilisene, which did no more than reaffirm the existing status quo in Armenia.

## Separation of 395

The Roman Empire underwent Christianization and was unified under the rule of Theodosius I. He was the last emperor to rule a unified empire. On his deathbed, he divided the empire. It's important to note that the empire remained divided until the fall of the Western Roman Empire. The division was a significant moment in the history of the Roman Empire since it marked the beginning of separate political and administrative entities.

The already fractured empire was split between Theodosius's sons. Honorius was appointed as the leader in the west, with the capital first in Milan and later in Ravenna. His territories included Italy, Gaul, North Africa, and a part of the Balkans. Arcadius encompassed eastern Europe, Macedonia, Egypt, Asia Minor, and Thrace, holding his power from the capital in Constantinople.

This formalization of separating the administration had been developing since the time of Diocletian in the late $3^{rd}$ and early $4^{th}$ century. This separation led to distinct political, cultural, and religious identities, eventually contributing to the fall of the Western Roman Empire and the flourishing of the Eastern Roman Empire.

Considering Arcadius was eighteen and Honorius only eleven years old, they were under the influence of their officials. In the Western Roman Empire, the real power was in the hands of Vandal Stilicho, a military commander close to Theodosius I.[1] Even though he was a Germanic barbarian, Stilicho was allowed to marry Serena, Theodosius's

---

[1] Mashkin, Nikolai, *A History of the Ancient Rome*, Gospolitizdat, 1956, p.406

niece, setting a precedent that allowed barbarian personnel to rise through the ranks.

The main threat came from the Visigoths, who were led by Alaric. Stilicho made a deal with Alaric but was killed soon after in 408. Alaric, who was of Germanic ancestry, once again proved that the Germanic tribes could acquire important positions. After Stilicho's death, Alaric attacked Rome and successfully sacked and pillaged the city in 410. It took him many attempts over the course of two years, but it is considered the final blow might have been possible with inside help from a slave or a Roman traitor.[i] For three days, the city was burned, destroyed, and raided. Even though he was Arian himself, Alaric spared the churches, allowing the Roman people a few safe spots during the havoc.[ii] Other buildings didn't share the same fate; an archaeological site in Aventine contains remains of buildings burned during this invasion.[iii]

Sack of Rome by Joseph-Noel Sylvestre (1890).[a]

---

[i] Bury, J.B. *The Invasion of Europe by the Barbarians*, W.W. Norton & Company, 2000, p.66
[ii] Mashkin, Nikolai, *A History of the Ancient Rome*, Gospolitizdat, 1956, p.406
[iii] Bury, J.B. *The Invasion of Europe by the Barbarians*, W.W. Norton & Company, 2000, p.67

The damaged empire was unable to resist fierce attacks from the Goths. Other parts of the empire began succumbing to their inevitable fate. Around 409, the Vandals and Alani took some parts of Spain. In 420, the Vandals solidified their position, and by 429, they had taken control of North Africa. The Huns, who were united by Attila in the 430s, posed a specially serious threat. The death of Emperor Honorius in 423 started a period of turmoil until the Eastern Roman government installed Valentinian II as the Western emperor in Ravenna.

Theodosius II, the new Eastern emperor and son of Arcadius, saw Aetius rise to the rank of magister militum.[i] Aetius was able to somewhat stabilize the military situation of the Western Empire. The Germanic general Ricimer succeeded Stilicho as a defender of the empire. Despite being German, these men proved to be capable of attaining the highest ranks and even married into the royal family. However, they were aware that as foreigners, they could never legally become rulers. During this time, the power lay in the Eastern Roman Empire.

## The Fall of Attila and the Huns

The Huns, led by Attila (434-453), pillaged and scourged the Balkans, causing the fall of many cities, such as Sirmium, Singidunum, Naissus, and Emona.[ii] Peace treaties were signed with Attila, but they were short-lived. After the death of Theodosius, his successor, Marcian, refused to pay the established fee to the Huns. Attila responded to this by sacking Gaul in 451. The Battle of Chalons, also known as the Battle of Maurica, occurred near the Catalaunian Plains.

The Roman forces were led by Flavius Aetius and faced a coalition of Hunnic and Germanic forces led by Attila. The battle involved tens of thousands of soldiers on both sides and resulted in heavy casualties. Although neither side achieved a decisive victory, the Romans managed to halt the Huns' advance. Attila later invaded Italy but was forced to retreat due to attacks by Marcian on the Danube.

Attila's sudden death in 453 did not prevent the deterioration of the Western Roman Empire. Chaos ensued even after the deaths of Aetius and Valentinian III. Petronius Maximus emerged as emperor, eventually

---

[i] Magister militum was a term that referred to a senior army commander with significant influence.
[ii] Romans perceived Attila as a divine punishment sent from Gods, giving him the nickname whip or scourge of God, referring to his brutal and fearsome reputation.

leading to the formation of new Germanic kingdoms in North Africa, Gaul, and Spain. The collapse of the Roman Empire was marked by the dominance of Germanic military leaders over ineffectual puppet emperors.

## New Battle Tactics of Eastern Armies

The Roman military strategy emphasized defensive warfare and the use of fortified positions. The army continued to utilize combined arms tactics, integrating infantry, cavalry, archers, and siege machines in coordinated maneuvers. Skilled commanders and disciplined troops proved to be good assets but had flaws. Byzantine commanders sometimes employed tactical deceptions, known as feigned flight. This required effective coordination and discipline but could be highly effective in surprising and defeating the enemy. Investing in the development of new systems and exploiting enemy weaknesses was useful in countering new threats that came in the coming centuries.

## The Collapse of the Western Roman Empire

The gradual collapse of the Western Roman Empire unfolded over several decades. While historians debate the exact causes and timeline, several key factors undoubtedly contributed to its downfall.

- Political instability and internal division: Frequent changes in leadership, often through assassination or usurpation, weakened central authority and hindered effective governance.
- Military decline: The once formidable military force gradually weakened due to budget cuts, corruption, and recruitment difficulties. Strained capabilities left the empire vulnerable to incursions by Germanic tribes, pressure from the Sasanian Persians, and the rise of the Huns.
- Economic crisis: High taxation, inflation, and corruption led to a downfall in trade and productivity, resulting in economic stagnation.
- Social unrest: Slave revolts, peasant uprisings, and urban unrest destabilized the empire, leading to the depopulation and decline of many cities while trade routes shifted.
- Loss of territory: Further invasions by Germanic tribes weakened the empire's strategic position, resulting in the loss of North Africa to the Vandals and Italy to the Ostrogoths.

Petronius Maximus was succeeded by other prominent generals, firstly Avitus and then by Ricimer. After the death of Ricimer in 472, it seemed his cousin Gundobad would inherit the leadership role. Gundobad couldn't come to an agreement with Eastern Emperor Leo (r. 457-474.). Leo's candidate was Julius Nepos. This conflict was resolved when Gundobad departed to Burgundy following his father's death. Julius Nepos was free to overtake the Western throne. He appointed Orestes, a former secretary of Attila, as magister militum while he himself retreated to Dalmatia.

Orestes crowned his young son as the new emperor with the name Romulus Augustus. Considering that Julius Nepos wasn't dead or overthrown, Romulus was not recognized by the Eastern court. Julius Nepos was still the legal emperor. In September 476, Odoacer, the leader of the Germanic *foederati* in Italy, seized Ravenna, killed Orestes, and deposed Romulus.[1] Julius Nepos did not return to Italy and continued to rule from Dalmatia, where he was in exile.

By law, there were still only two legitimate emperors, Zeno in the East and Julius Nepos in the West. Romulus Augustus was an illegitimate sovereign who was overthrown in a coup, but he never objected to Zeno's power. Odoacer accepted Zeno and eventually invaded Dalmatia after the murder of Julius Nepos in 480. Zeno abolished the title and position of the Western Roman emperor and assumed the role of Odoacer's sovereign. Odoacer was simultaneously the king of the Goths as well as the magister militum.

The position of the Roman emperor would never again be divided, though some candidates for the Western emperor position were proposed in the 6th century. After the Western Roman Empire crumbled, various Germanic tribes led Italy and its provinces. The new Germanic rulers maintained most of the Roman laws and traditions, and many tribes were Christianized, although they mostly followed Arianism.

---

[1] The foederati were tribes bound by a treaty.

# Chapter 4: Justinian's Dream of Restoration

## *Renovatio imperii*: Reconquering the West

Emperor Zeno's reign (r. 474-475 and 476-491) was defined by internal revolts and religious conflicts. His successor, Anastasius I (r. 491-518), tried to stabilize the economy and implement financial reforms. Although known for his construction projects, his rule was not very successful. Justin I, an elderly officer, was chosen as emperor after Anastasius I passed away and remained on the throne until his death in 527. These emperors set the stage for Justinian I, who would go on to have a profound impact on the Byzantine Empire and the lands beyond. Justin's reign focused on internal stability and preparing his nephew Justinian for succession.

Justinian was born to a peasant family of either Illyro-Roman or Thraco-Roman origin. The name *Iustinianus* was indicative of his adoption by his uncle Justin, who brought him to Constantinople and looked after his education. Others who contributed to Justinian's success included his finance ministers, John the Cappadocian and Peter Barsymes, who collected taxes more efficiently than anyone before, funding the wars that his talented generals Belisarius and Narses led. Justinian's reign is known for his ambitious but only partly realized idea of *renovatio imperii* ("restoration of the empire"). Justinian rose through the ranks of the Byzantine bureaucracy and became a close advisor to Emperor Justin I. In 527, he was named co-emperor, and shortly after, his uncle died, leaving him to become the sole emperor at the age of forty-five.

During Justinian's rule, the Eastern Roman Empire managed to overcome the crisis that had led to the fall of the Western Roman Empire. Justinian was instrumental in shaping the empire's policies during this time. A noteworthy aspect of his reign was the reconquest of the western Mediterranean. As a Christian and a great connoisseur of Roman history, he felt it was his divine duty to restore the Roman Empire to its ancient boundaries.

A map depicting Justinian's expansion to the west.[9]

The first of the western kingdoms Justinian targeted was the Vandal Kingdom in North Africa. King Hilderic, who had maintained good relations with Justinian, was overthrown by his cousin Gelimer in 530. This event prompted Justinian to demand the return of the kingdom to Hilderic.

Justinian inherited ongoing hostilities with the Sasanian Empire from his predecessors. In 530, the Persian forces suffered defeats at Dara and Satala, while the Romans faced a loss near Callincium. Justinian attempted to form alliances with the Axumites of Ethiopia and the Himyarites of Yemen and lay a final blow to the Persians, but these efforts were unsuccessful.

After Gelimer refused his demands to return the Vandal Kingdom to Hilderic, Justinian knew he had to secure one of the frontiers. Following the death of King Kavadh I of Persia in 531, Justinian established an "eternal peace" with Kavadh's successor, Khosrow, in 532. With the eastern frontier secured, he turned his attention to the west, where Germanic tribes had been established for decades.

Justinian prepared an expedition against the Vandals in 533. The emperor's trusted general Belisarius sailed to Africa with a fleet of ninety-two dromons (a type of galley) and five hundred transports carrying a large number of men, counting up to eighteen thousand.[i] The forces landed in modern-day Tunisia and caught the Vandals off guard, defeating them at Ad Decimum in September and Tricamarum in December of the same year. Belisarius captured Carthage, and King Gelimer, who initially fled, surrendered the following year. Gelimer was taken to Constantinople, where he was paraded during a triumph. Word of Belisarius's plan to proclaim himself as king of Africa could be heard throughout the empire but was overshadowed by the glorious parade.

In the same campaign, Belisarius also recovered Sardinia and Corsica, as well as the Balearic Islands and the stronghold of Septem Fratres (later named Gibraltar). Although the area was not completely pacified until 548, it remained peaceful and experienced a measure of prosperity.

As in Africa, dynastic struggles in Ostrogothic Italy provided an opportunity for intervention. The young king Athalaric had died in 534, and the usurper Theodahad had imprisoned and assassinated the widowed queen Amalasuintha, the mother of Athalaric. So, Belisarius invaded Sicily and advanced to Italy, sacking Naples and capturing Rome in December 536. By that time, Theodahad had been deposed by the army, which elected its commander, Vitigis (also spelled Vitiges), as the new king. Vitigis gathered a large army and besieged Rome for over a year between 537 and 538.

His efforts weren't enough to retake the city. Justinian sent Narses to aid Belisarius, but tensions between them hampered the campaign's progress. Milan was taken but soon recaptured by the Ostrogoths. Not very long after that setback, Justinian recalled Narses to settle the tensions between the two generals. By 540, Belisarius had reached the Ostrogothic capital Ravenna. The Ostrogoths tried to lure Belisarius to their side by giving him the title of Western Roman emperor. He feigned acceptance and entered the city to reclaim it for Justinian.

In the face of renewed hostilities by the Persians, Belisarius was recalled to the eastern front. King Khosrow I broke the eternal peace and invaded Roman territory in the spring of 540. The following years were characterized by upsets on Roman territory. Justinian suffered some

---

[i] Ostrogorsky, George, *History of the Byzantine State,* Rutgers University Press, 1969, p..89.

defeats and lost a few smaller quarrels.

While military efforts were directed to the east, the situation in Italy took a turn for the worse once again. Under their respective kings, Ildibad, Eraric, and Totila, the Ostrogoths made quick gains in the lands not secured by Justinian I. They reconquered some major cities and almost managed to take the entire Italian Peninsula. Belisarius was sent back to Italy in 544, but he lacked troops and supplies after the clash with the Persians. After making no progress, he was relieved of his command in 548. During these four years, Rome changed hands many times between the Ostrogoths and Byzantines. Finally, Justinian dispatched a large force of approximately thirty-five thousand men under the command of Narses. In 552, they reached Ravenna and defeated the Ostrogoths decisively at the Battle of Busta Gallorum (Battle of Taginae), where Totila was slain. There was another smaller battle to finish the Ostrogoth resistance. In 554, a large-scale Frankish invasion was defeated at Casilinum, and Italy was secured for the empire. It would take Narses several more years of continuous efforts to reduce the remaining Gothic strongholds in occasional smaller clashes.

In addition, the Byzantine Empire established a presence in Visigothic Hispania, where the usurper Athanagild requested assistance in his rebellion against King Agila I. The Byzantines took Cartagena and other cities on the southeastern coast and founded the new province of Spania. The newly crowned king of the Visigoths acknowledged the suzerainty of the empire, which marked the highest point in Byzantine expansion.

In the end, Justinian's ambitions were only partly realized, with noteworthy sustainable conquests in Africa. In the West, the successes of the 530s were followed by years of stagnation. The dragging feuds with the Goths were a disaster for Italy. The enlarged area of Byzantine influence eliminated naval threats, and the empire reached its territorial zenith in 555.[1] Truth be told, not every ex-Roman territory was under Justinian's rule, but having conquered North Africa, Spain, and Italy, he once again made the Mediterranean Sea a "Roman lake."

---

[1] Ostrogorsky, George, *History of the Byzantine State,* Rutgers University Press, 1969, p.89.

A mosaic of Emperor Justinian in the Basilica of San Vitale, Ravenna.[10]

## Nika Riots

Justinian's rule was not universally popular. He almost lost the throne during the Nika riots, and a conspiracy against his life was discovered as late as 562. Amidst turbulent external affairs, internal unrest flared up rapidly. Heated altercations between the autocratic centralized government and various political organizations divided the empire.

The riots were sparked by social, political, and sporting rivalries that had been building up for some time. The two main factions involved were the Blues and the Greens, names that originated from chariot racing teams but also represented broader factions within the city.[i] Although Justinian was fond of the Blues in the beginning, his support abated once he took a more neutral stance and sought to limit the power of all the factions. Contrary to Anastasius I, Justinian wanted to free himself of the deme's influence and imposed punitive measures on fighting organizations.[ii]

---

[i] There were initially four factions: Blue (*Veneti*), Green (*Prasini*), Red (*Russati*), and White (*Albati*), but by the 6th century, most of the influence was distributed between the Blues and Greens.

[ii] In ancient Athens, *deme* was a municipality. In the Byzantine Empire, however, *deme* signified the chariot racing factions (perhaps based on municipal borders), as well as political factions that formed around these groups, such as the Blues and Greens.

As early as January 532, unrest arose in Constantinople at the Hippodrome during a chariot race. Unsatisfied attendees yelled, "Nika" ("win," "triumph," or "conquer"), a chant that would become the symbol and the name of these riots.[i]

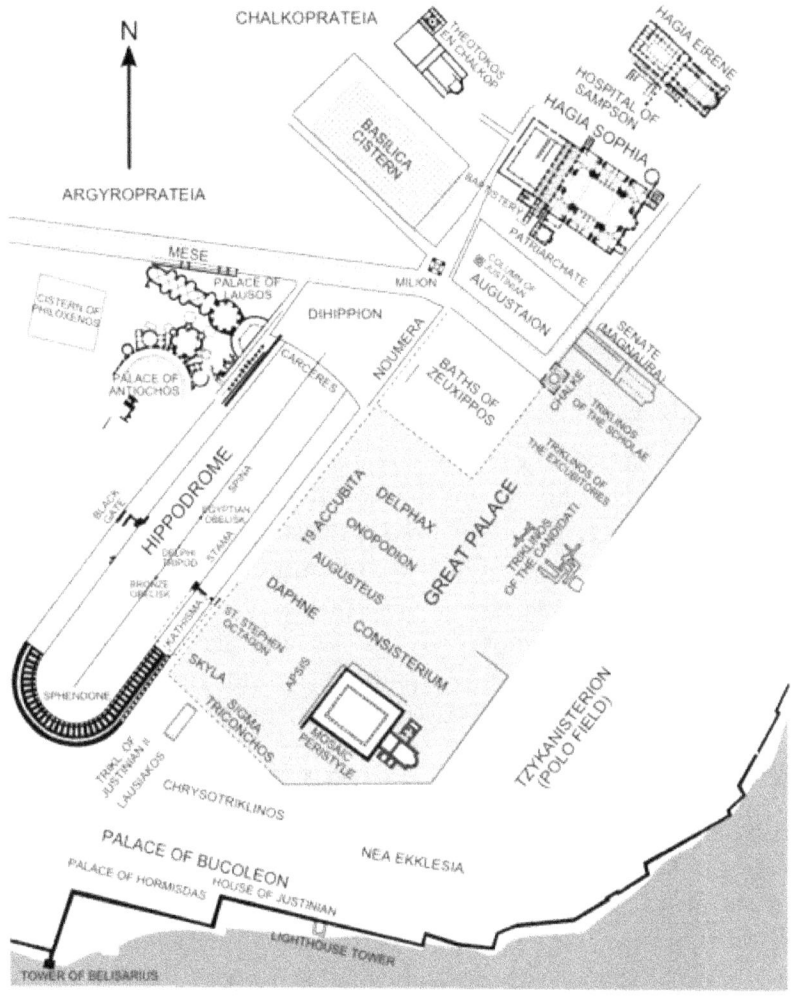

A map of the palace and Hippodrome during the riots.[ii]

The riots began as a verbal protest but quickly escalated into widespread violence and chaos. Soon, the capital of the empire was engulfed in flames. Most notably, Hagia Sophia, the Praetorium, and the

---

[i] Mitchell, Stephen, *A History of the Later Roman Empire AD 284-641*, Oxford: Blackwell, 2007, p.198.

city's main granaries were set ablaze. The united rioters proclaimed Hypatius, Anastasius's nephew, as the new emperor, which incited Justinian to contemplate fleeing the city. Empress Theodora was the one who convinced him to stay, while Belisarius and Nerses managed to break the unity of the protesters.[i]

The commanders moved into the Hippodrome and trapped the rioters. Narses tried to bribe the Blue faction, reminding them that Justinian was fond of them and also mentioning that Hypatius was a sympathizer of the Greens in order to divide them. Blinded by the gold, the voracious rioters were caught off guard when Belisarius began killing anyone left in the Hippodrome, whether they were Blue or Green supporters. Hypatius and his associates were also killed during the carnage. This "maneuver" in the Hippodrome marked the end of the uprising. Justinian used the opportunity to consolidate his power and undertook significant reforms and construction projects, including rebuilding the burned Hagia Sophia.

This riot was a pivotal event in Byzantine history, as it shaped the reign of Justinian and the subsequent development of the entire empire. This bloodbath took thirty thousand lives and remains the most controversial aspect of Justinian's rule.[ii] One of the more interesting things is the importance Justinian attached to this episode. He announced victory by proclaiming he had removed tyrants from all the cities, obviously exaggerating the magnitude of the outcome. Justinian emerged as a more confident and sterner ruler after this success.

## The Great Hagia Sophia

Whether it was fate or projected unrest, the events that transpired in the city gave the emperor a chance to stamp his mark deeper on the capital. The main project he focused on was the church known as Hagia Sophia, which was not only the most spectacular church of late antiquity but also inspired Christian and Muslim architectural traditions in the centuries to come. Justinian enlisted architects Isidore of Miletus and Anthemius of Tralles for the restoration. The shape of the church shifted the focus from the cross toward the dome as a representation of the sky and a symbol of the divine. Materials were brought from every part of the empire.

---

[i] Ostrogorsky, George, *History of the Byzantine State,* Rutgers University Press, 1969, p. 91.
[ii] Mitchell, Stephen, *A History of the Later Roman Empire AD 284-641*, Oxford: Blackwell, 2007, p. 194.

Considering the scale of the project and the technology of the time, it is surprising that the construction took only five years to complete. The dedication ceremony was grand and attended by Justinian, a multitude of clergy, and the citizens of Constantinople and other parts of the empire.

The knowledge about domes at the time was not advanced enough, resulting in its collapse in 558. During Justinian's final years of rule, the newly upgraded dome was finished and is standing to this day as part of the mosque in what is now Istanbul. This achievement exemplifies Justinian's ambition and dedication to restore Constantinople as the center of the Roman Empire and to leave his mark on the history of the empire.

## Empress Theodora

Mosaic of Empress Theodora in the Basilica of San Vitale, Ravenna.[12]

Empress Theodora's early life is characterized by humble beginnings. Her father was a bear trainer at the Hippodrome and an ally to the Green faction, but after his death, Theodora's favor shifted toward the Blues. Her acting career gave her access to influential circles and brought her to the attention of Justinian, who was the heir to the throne.

Procopius colorfully wrote that Theodora made a name for herself with her pornographic portrayal of Leda and the Swan.[i] The accuracy of Procopius's portrayal is unclear because sexual promiscuity was ascribed to many females of low origin or who had acting careers. It was rumored she was a dancer in brothels instead of being an actress, but despite conventions and prejudices, Justinian wanted to marry her. A law that had been in power since Constantine I barred anyone of senatorial rank from marrying an actress. But in 524, Justinian passed a law allowing reformed actresses to marry outside their rank if approved by the emperor. In 525, he married Theodora. This marriage caused a scandal and inspired animosity toward her, though she became very influential in the politics of the empire later on.

After Justinian succeeded the throne in 527, she was crowned Augusta and became empress against all odds. She shared Justinian's vision that there could be no Roman empire that did not include Rome itself. Being relatively young as an emperor and empress compared to their predecessors, they weren't content to maintain the status quo. During the Nika riots, her role was of vital importance to the outcome and Justinian's decision-making. She persuaded him not to flee and to take a stand. According to Procopius (a source not to be believed blindly), she interrupted the emperor and his counselors to motivate them with a speech.[ii]

Theodora was known for her intelligence and political savvy. She often advocated for policies that benefited the lower classes and worked to curb the power of the aristocracy. She was very involved in helping underprivileged women. Theodora championed the rights of women and enacted laws to protect them, such as protection for women against abusive husbands. She bought girls sold into prostitution and freed them, providing for their future. In 528, she ordered the closure of brothels and arrested keepers and procurers. This probably reflected the remorse she had regarding her (alleged) past choices.

Her death is recorded by Victor of Tunnuna, and the cause is uncertain, but many believe it to have been a serious illness.[iii] Theodora

---

[i] A story from Greek mythology in which the god Zeus seduces a Spartan queen in the form of a swan.

[ii] Procopius, *The Secret History*, Penguin Books, 1982, p. 38.

[iii] A bishop from North Africa and a chronicler of the time known for his outward resistance toward Justinian I.

was known for her strong sympathy toward the Miaphysite Christians, who rejected the Chalcedonian definition of Christ having two distinct natures. Although Justinian remained officially committed to Chalcedonian orthodoxy, he made significant efforts later in his reign to reconcile the two factions, efforts that many historians believe were influenced by Theodora, even after her death in 548.

The imperial couple is famously depicted in the mosaics of the Basilica of San Vitale in Ravenna, completed around 547, shortly before Theodora's death.

## Law and Administration

Justinian was known as "the emperor who never sleeps" for his devotion to the empire. He achieved lasting fame through his judicial reforms, particularly the complete revision of all Roman law, something not previously attempted. Justinian's law and administration are among his most enduring legacies, influencing legal systems to this day. His legislation is now known as the *Corpus Juris Civilis* (Body of Civil Law). The *Corpus Juris Civilis* consists of several components, the most important of which are the following:

1. **Codex Justinianus** – The Codex Justinianus (Code of Justinian) was a collection of imperial enactments and laws issued by previous emperors known as Theodosian, Gregorian, and Hermogenian codices organized thematically and intended to simplify and update existing laws. Early in his reign, Justinian appointed the quaestor Tribonian to oversee this task. The first draft of the Codex Justinianus was issued in 529 and then again five years later as a supplemented edition.[i]

2. **Digesta** (or **Pandects**) – The Digesta was a compilation of legal opinions and writings published in 533. Classical Roman jurists were often contradictory to one another, and for the first time, their works were systematically reviewed and organized in a more functional way.

3. **Institutes** – The *Institutes* was a textbook that served as an introduction to Roman law for law students, ensuring future law representatives would have a better understanding of implemented changes.

---

[i] Ostrogorsky, George, *History of the Byzantine State,* Rutgers University Press, 1969, p. 94.

4. **Novellae Constitutiones** (or **Justinian's Novels**) – These were new laws or amendments issued by Justinian himself after the completion of the codex. While the Codex Justinianus, Digesta, and *Institutes* were published in Latin, *Justinian's Novels* were written in Greek. Justinian decided the other three parts should also be translated into Greek and spread across the empire in both languages.[i]

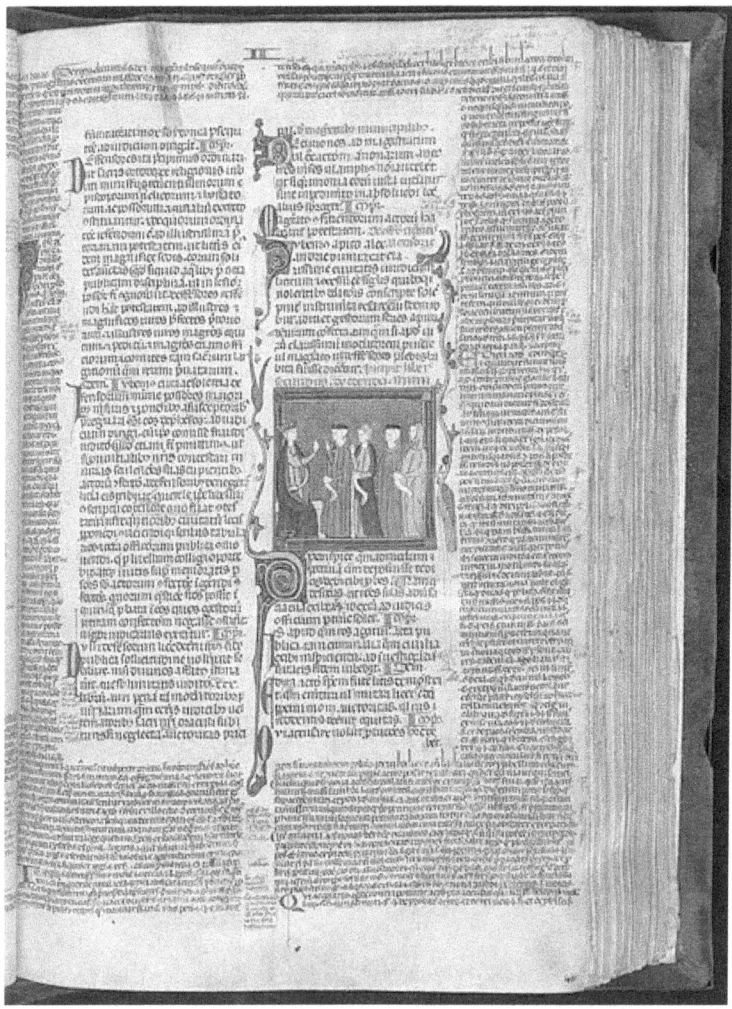

Medieval copy of the famous Code of Justinian, copied by Franciscus Accursius in the 13th century. Preserved in the Ghent University Library.[18]

---

[i] Ibid.

By participating in different parts of the empire's legal system, Justinian succeeded in his attempt to untangle obsolete law codices. The codification of Roman law provided a strong legal foundation for the centralized state. It outlined regulations for public and private life and societal and family matters while also aligning them with Christian ideals and morals with notable Hellenistic influences.

In 541, there was a discontinuation of the regular appointment of consuls. The empire's social welfare program aimed to prevent hunger, with free bread provided at twenty state bakeries and free access to public baths for all residents. Additionally, the Byzantine administration was reorganized to enhance efficiency and centralization. Skilled administrators and legal experts were appointed to key positions to streamline governance and improve tax collection. Provinces were grouped into larger administrative units called dioceses, each under the control of a governor.

# Part Two:
# From Latin to Greek Empires
# (565–867 CE)

# Chapter 5: New Enemies at the Gates

The great conquests of Emperor Justinian restored the glory and power of the former Roman Empire and once again turned the Mediterranean Sea into a "Roman lake." The Byzantine Empire utilized all its available resources to allow the old empire to experience its final political and cultural resurgence.[i] The territorial expansion to the west was successful, and there was a flourishing in literature and art. Justinian's efforts failed to restore the empire, but it briefly and superficially revived the splendor of the aging Roman state apparatus.

With his grand endeavors, Justinian aimed to start a new era in the empire's history, but he did the opposite, causing its final collapse and transformation. The territorial restoration of the Roman Empire lacked a solid foundation and internal reforms, leading to its disintegration by the end of Justinian's reign. The empire he left to his successors was internally exhausted and economically and financially shaken due to extensive military undertakings. Justinian left a vast empire that could not be defended, so subsequent rulers had to correct all of the great emperor's mistakes and salvage what could be saved.[ii]

Justinian sacrificed certain border territories in the east and along the Danube limes through his military and financial efforts in the policy of

---

[i] Ibid
[ii] Runciman, *Byzantine Civilization*.

western expansion.[i] The Sasanian dynasty in Persia, led by Khosrow I (r. 531-579), managed to capture a large amount of Byzantine territory in northern Mesopotamia and Armenia at the beginning of Justinian's reign.[ii] However, Justinian's famed general Belisarius managed to gain the upper hand in the war, resulting in the so-called "eternal peace." The Persians broke the peace in 540, taking advantage of the Byzantine army's engagement in Italy. They crossed the border and captured Antioch in Syria. Persia's breakthrough to the Mediterranean was crowned with a ritual bath of Khosrow I in the Mediterranean Sea and the offering of sacrifices. The imperial army, with great effort, managed to defend the crucial fortress of Dara and forced the Persians to withdraw from Edessa and retreat from Syria. Another peace treaty was signed in Dara in 562 called the Fifty-Year Peace, and Justinian spent the final years of his reign with peaceful borders in the East.[iii]

## After Justinian

Justinian's successors inevitably shifted the focus of their policy toward the East, with the primary task of consolidating the empire's weakened position in central Asia. A firm stance toward Persia became a characteristic feature of Byzantine policy over the next few decades. The peace that had financially and militarily cost Byzantium so much was disrupted by Justinian's nephew, Justin II (r. 565-578), who, in 572, stopped paying the agreed tribute to Persia.

The entourage around the emperor advised exploiting the troubles in Persia and extending Byzantine influence over all of Armenia. Turkish tribes invaded northern Persia, devastating the region, which encouraged the Caucasian Iberians and Armenians to revolt against Khosrow in alliance with Justin II. Emperor Justin II sent his commander Marcian to gather an army in the east and station them at the fortress of Dara. Supported by the Iberians and Armenians, he attacked the Persian city of Nisibis in Mesopotamia.

Before the decisive clash with Khosrow's approaching army, Emperor Justin II ordered a change in command and transferred all of Marcian's authority to Acacius, who failed to organize the army. Due to a

---

[i] A lime is a border separating the empire from barbarian lands.

[ii] Ostrogorsky, *History of the Byzantine State*.

[iii] Ibid.

communication and command error, the military collapsed, and the Persians ravaged the Byzantine province of Syria and reached the Mediterranean again. This time, the Byzantines lost their famous fortress, Dara.

News of the catastrophic defeat reached Constantinople in 574 and further deteriorated the already shaken mental health of Emperor Justin II. Meanwhile, Khosrow continued to devastate Byzantine territories in the northeast. The war with Persia was continued by Justin II's successor, the energetic Emperor Maurice (r. 582-602), but this time, he managed to take advantage of the unrest that broke out in Persia. With his support, the young Khosrow II Parviz (r. 590-628), grandson of Khosrow I, ascended to the Persian throne. Maurice succeeded in securing peace by signing a treaty with the young Khosrow in 591, regaining the lost territories.[i]

## The Italian Situation

The heaviest blow to Byzantium occurred in Italy, the most important region of the restored empire whose reoccupation had required great efforts and sacrifices. Pressured by the Avars, the Lombards invaded Italy in 568 and quickly conquered a large part of it. Alboin (r. c. 560-572), the Lombard king, united the major Germanic tribes in an alliance with the Lombards and defeated the Gepid Kingdom of King Cunimund in the Pannonian Plain. Due to the significant pressure from the advancing Avars, he had to retreat from Pannonia to the old Roman province of Raetia, where he waited for a better opportunity to invade war-ravaged Italy.

In the first months of 568, a large group, mainly consisting of the Lombards, penetrated into Italy, swiftly capturing cities like Padua, Mantua, and Cremona. The famous Byzantine general Narses was tasked with defending Italy in the Po Valley, but he was around ninety years old, and his army and subordinates were unable to stop the conquests.[ii] The only city that offered more resilient resistance was Pavia, which held out against the Lombards for three years but eventually surrendered in 571. With the fall of Pavia, King Alboin controlled half of Italy, which he divided into thirteen Lombard duchies.

---

[i] Ibid.
[ii] Bury, *A History of the Later Roman Empire*.

# Africa

In North Africa, the Byzantine Empire maintained its position despite constant exhausting battles with the Moorish tribes until the Arab invasion. Even in Italy, provinces remained under Byzantine rule for several centuries.[i] Thus, the remnants of Justinian's conquests long formed the foundation on which Byzantine power in the West rested. However, the aspiration for world domination vanished forever.

Emperor Maurice (r. 582-602), unlike Justin II, was a statesman of high caliber. Through shrewd policies in the East, he secured the long-needed peace but had to relinquish territories in the West that the Germanic peoples were beginning to conquer. During Maurice's reign, significant measures were taken to preserve Byzantine authority in the newly conquered regions. By reforming the state apparatus in the remnants of these areas, military governorships were established: the Exarchate of Ravenna, which included the remaining Byzantine holdings in Italy, and the Exarchate of Carthage, which encompassed the North African coast. Because of their strong military organization, the exarchates were capable of defense and became the vanguard of Byzantine power in the West. Exarchs, the governors, were in charge of both military and civil administration in their territories. The establishment of the exarchates in Ravenna and Carthage marked the beginning of the Byzantine administration's militarization. The organization of the exarchates would later serve as a model for the arrangement of themes, which were administrative districts of the Byzantine Empire (the region of modern-day Turkey was at one point divided into more than a dozen themes).[ii]

# Iberia

Right from the start, Byzantine holdings in the Iberian Peninsula were attacked by their former Visigothic rulers. Visigothic Kings Athanagild and Leovigild conquered the interior territories of the province of Spain, reducing Byzantine control to the coastal areas along the Mediterranean. Many territories were lost during King Leovigild's offensives in 571 and 577, but the Byzantines continued to control key cities in the region of Baetica, such as Carthago Nova, and occasionally reclaimed lost areas. Emperor Maurice managed to consolidate the remaining territories of the

---

[i] Ostrogorsky, *History of the Byzantine State*.
[ii] Ibid

province of Spain and signed a peace treaty with King Reccared I of the Visigoths (r. 586-601) through the mediation of Pope Gregory I the Great. However, the province of Spain did not undergo the exarchate reforms like other territories due to the difficulties in maintaining it and its distance from Constantinople.

After the violent death of Emperor Maurice and the turmoil in the Byzantine Empire, the Visigoths took a firmer stance toward the Byzantine holdings. Over the next twenty years, they managed to conquer all the cities and reclaim their former territories in the Iberian Peninsula except for the Balearic Islands, which were later conquered by the Arabs.[i]

## The Balkans

The preoccupation of Justinian's troops with conquests in the West and the defensive policy toward Persia in the East left the Danubian frontier undefended. Even during the reign of Justinian's predecessor, Emperor Justin I, the Antes launched an attack on Byzantine territories. In the early years of Justinian's reign, the Slavic tribes, in alliance with the Bulgars, began continuous incursions into the Balkan provinces. In response, Emperor Justinian erected an entire system of fortifications along the Danube and in the interior of the threatened provinces.[ii] However, the defense of the frontier lacked manpower rather than fortifications. While the Byzantine army celebrated its great victories in the West, the Slavs flooded the Balkan Peninsula from the Adriatic to the Aegean and from the Danube to the Gulf of Corinth.

The Slavs were initially content with plundering the central Byzantine provinces, transporting the loot across the Danube into their territories. Over time, Slavic migrations began to spread into the interior of Byzantium, marking an era of constant Slavic settlement in the Balkan Peninsula.

The tumultuous state of the Byzantine Empire due to frequent Slavic incursions across the Sava and the Danube was further exacerbated by the appearance of the Avars in the Pannonian Plain. According to the Byzantine historian Menander, the Avars established their state (khaganate) under the rule of Khagan Bayan, who governed large groups of Slavs. Byzantium now faced a new formidable enemy on its Danubian

---

[i] Bury, *The Invasion of Europe by the Barbarians*.
[ii] Ostrogorsky, *History of the Byzantine State*.

borders who coordinated attacks on its territories. Bitter battles began over crossings of the Sava and the Danube with the aim of capturing the first major stronghold and former imperial city of Sirmium. Sirmium was besieged in 579 and managed to hold out for the next three years, but unfortunately for Byzantium, Emperor Tiberius II Constantine (r. 574-582) failed to secure peace through diplomatic means.[i] The city fell into Avar hands in 582 after the emperor's death, becoming a base for further incursions into the empire's interior.

While the Avars besieged border fortresses, Slavs from the central Danubian region, following Bayan's orders, plundered Hellas in 580. Slavic tribes settled in the former Roman province of Dacia ravaged the territory of Thrace. According to the Byzantine historian Theophylact Simocatta, these Slavic tribes were not subordinate to Bayan and independently carried out raids. Simocatta refers to their territory as Sclavinia.[ii] Two years after the conquest of Sirmium, the Avars captured Singidunum, which would change hands multiple times. In the same year, 584, Viminacium and Augusta also fell, dismantling the Byzantine defensive system and allowing the Avars and Slavs to spread across the Balkan Peninsula. In the following years, 584 and 586, the first Avar-Slavic attack on Thessalonica occurred, and more importantly, the permanent settlement of certain Slavic tribes in Byzantine territories began. The Slavs were no longer content with just plundering. They transitioned into a sedentary way of life, occupying territories on Byzantine soil.

---

[i] Diehl, *History of the Byzantine Empire*.
[ii] Bury, *The Invasion of Europe by the Barbarians*.

Migration of Slavs in the early medieval age.[14]

## Foreign Policy and the Internal Situation

Among the significant foreign policy changes of the early Byzantine period, none had nearly as much impact on the Byzantine Empire as the penetration of the Slavs into the Balkans. All other barbarian incursions that the empire experienced at that time were transient. Even the great migration of the Germans, which shook the empire profoundly, ultimately bypassed Byzantium. In contrast, the Slavs remained in the Balkans permanently, greatly influencing Byzantine history.[i]

By saving territories in the West and engaging in constant wars with Persia in the East, Justinian's successors failed to take any action to save Byzantine possessions in the Balkans. Only after the victorious conclusion of the war with Persia in 591 did Emperor Maurice (r. 582-602) manage to transfer a significant portion of the army from the East and initiate an offensive against the Slavs in the Danube region. Maurice appointed his generals who had distinguished themselves in the Persian War, such as Comentiolus, who was tasked with defending the interior territories, and

---

[i] Ostrogorsky, *History of the Byzantine State*.

the strategos (general) Priscus, who was to defeat the Slavs from the other side of the Danube.

In 594, Priscus launched a major raid into Slavic territories (Sclavinia), where, according to sources, he managed to kill one of the Slavic leaders and return with significant spoils of war. The following year, Maurice's brother, the curopalates Peter, led the Byzantine army in an incursion into Slavic territories, successfully disrupting their organization, recovering plundered Byzantine treasures, and capturing a leader.[i]

In addition to the campaigns against the Slavs, Maurice ordered his generals Priscus and Comentiolus to penetrate the Avar Khaganate in 597 and 599, thereby inflicting the first defeat on the Avars deep within their territory.[ii] The struggle dragged on, leading to a war in the remote Danube region, which was difficult and exhausting. There was no significant impact on the large masses of Slavs, causing the combativeness of the Byzantine army to decline.

After the collapse of Justinian's restoration, Byzantium lost much of its authority. In reaction to Justinian's absolutism, the political importance of the Senate increased, and the urban population's desire for freedom grew. Discipline in the army greatly declined, often leading to open manifestations of dissatisfaction, especially as the government frequently delayed soldiers' pay.

## Rebellion

In 602, the curopalates Peter was tasked by Emperor Maurice to lead the army across the Danube, but a rebellion broke out. The rebellious soldiers acclaimed Phocas, a man with barbarian origins, as emperor. The army then abandoned its positions and marched on Constantinople after an uprising supported by the Senate erupted in the city. Emperor Maurice was deposed and executed in the square with his supporters, and the Senate crowned Phocas as the new emperor in Constantinople. The collapse of the Byzantine army on the Danube, after a futile ten-year struggle, sealed the fate of the Balkan Peninsula, which was left to the Slavs.

---

[i] Curopalates was a court title. It formally designated a person who was in charge of handling imperial palace matters. Females could rise to the rank of courapalates.

[ii] Bury, *The Invasion of Europe by the Barbarians*.

Byzantium faced a catastrophe that had long been postponed by the struggles of the previous decades. The complete collapse of Byzantine defensive strength occurred both in the Balkans and in the east toward Persia. The Persians crossed the border and penetrated deep into Asia Minor up to Caesarea (modern-day Israel) after capturing the fortress of Dara in 605. During this time, the Balkans again fell into turmoil due to Slavic-Avar incursions. Not even Phocas increasing the tribute to the Avars helped. Soon, the entire Balkan Peninsula was flooded with enormous Slavic masses, and the entire Byzantine Empire found itself on the brink of collapse.[i]

The years of anarchy under Phocas marked both the final years of the old empire and the end of the post-Roman early Byzantine era. After the severe crisis experienced by Byzantium, it would emerge as a new state under the new emperor, Heraclius (r. 610–641). It was liberated from the decaying post-Roman state and strengthened by new forces.[ii] Now, the true history of Byzantium begins, or rather, the history of the medieval Greek empire.

Depiction of Heraclius on a coin.[14]

---

[i] Ostrogorsky, *History of the Byzantine State*.
[ii] Ibid.

# Chapter 6: The Arab Invasion

After the conclusion of the first major religious war of the Christian era, the Byzantine-Sasanian War (602-628), Emperor Heraclius managed to completely destroy the power of the Persian state and reclaim all territories that belonged to Byzantium.[i] As the enemy evacuated from Byzantine provinces, Heraclius symbolically returned the Holy Cross to Jerusalem and celebrated a victory in the spring of 630.[ii]

Amidst this great war, which had repercussions for all states and peoples located east of Byzantium, Muhammad laid the foundations for a new religious and political unity in the Arab world. Muhammad's persona and deeds injected a new driving force among the numerous tribes of the Arabian Peninsula. In the same years when Heraclius celebrated his triumph in Jerusalem, Muhammad triumphantly entered Mecca. Just a few years after the Prophet's death, a great Arab migration began.[iii] They abandoned their barren territory and advanced unstoppably, subjugating neighboring peoples. Their initial goal was not the spread of Islam but rather the conquest of new lands.

---

[i] Howard-Johnston, *East Rome, Sasanian Persia and the End of Antiquity*.
[ii] Diehl, *History of the Byzantine Empire*.
[iii] Kennedy, *The Great Arab Conquests*.

# The Rise of the Arabs

The centuries-long struggle between Byzantium and Persia weakened both empires, thus facilitating the rise of a new religious and state entity: the Rashidun Caliphate.[i] The Rashidun ("rightly guided") Caliphate was the first Islamic state established after the death of the Prophet Muhammad. His four immediate successors and close companions—Abu Bakr, Umar, Uthman, and Ali—held the title of caliph and significantly expanded the Islamic state through military conquests and administrative reforms. It lasted from Muhammad's death in 632 to 661, when it was succeeded by the Umayyad Caliphate.

The first major victim of their onslaught was the defeated Sasanian Empire, which was engulfed in chaos. A civil war broke out among the sons of Khosrow II after the defeat in the Battle of Nineveh and the Byzantine conquest of the capital. The eldest son, Sheroe (Kavad II), led a conspiracy that resulted in the death of his father and half-brother, and then he crowned himself as Kavad II. The situation in the Persian realm allowed the renowned Arab commander Khalid ibn al-Walid to, upon the order of Caliph Abu Bakr (r. 632-634), launch the first incursion into Sasanian territories in 633. He captured a large part of Mesopotamia and subjugated the Lakhmid Kingdom.[ii]

In the years following the initial Arab incursions, the Muslim armies were engaged on multiple fronts, including their ongoing conflict with the Byzantine Empire. In a decisive campaign, General Saʿd ibn Abī Waqqāṣ led a victorious army at the Battle of al-Qādisiyyah in 636, which resulted in the permanent Arab conquest of Mesopotamia and the collapse of Sasanian control over the region. The new frontier was eventually established along the Zagros Mountains, marking the loss of the western territories of the Sasanian Empire.[iii]

The conquest of Persia continued under Caliph Umar (r. 634-644) when a great victory was won at the Battle of Nahavand in 642, resulting in the subjugation of the entire territory of the great Sasanian Empire in the following years.[iv] The last king from the Sasanian dynasty, Yazdegerd III, was killed in 651, and his relatives found refuge in China. Under Caliph

---

[i] Howard-Johnston, *East Rome, Sasanian Persia and the End of Antiquity*.
[ii] Nicolle, *The Great Islamic Conquests, AD 632-750*.
[iii] Kennedy, *The Great Arab Conquests*.
[iv] Nicolle, *The Great Islamic Conquests, AD 632-750*.

Uthman (r. 644-656), the caliphate had expanded in the east to the border with India in less than twenty years.[i]

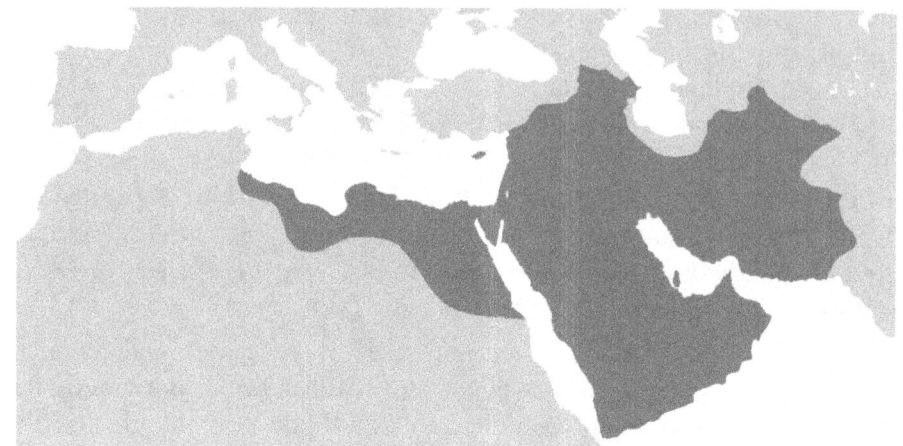

The Rashidun Caliphate in the mid-7ᵗʰ century CE.[16]

Unlike Persia, the victorious Byzantine army was exhausted by the long and arduous war that was being fought on multiple fronts. Within the empire, religious tensions were prevalent along the stretch from Constantinople to the eastern provinces. These tensions fueled aspirations among the Coptic and Syrian populations, which undermined the defensive ability of these regions.

Two years after Muhammad's death in 634, the Arabs invaded the Byzantine Empire under the leadership of Caliph Umar (r. 634-644) and rapidly advanced through the territories of the Ghassanids (modern-day Syria, roughly speaking) and the recently reclaimed provinces from the Persians. The battle that would herald the further expansion of the Arab army and the complete collapse of Byzantine defenses took place at the Yarmouk River on August 20ᵗʰ, 636.[ii,iii] The Byzantines lost this fateful battle, enabling the Arabs to conquer all of Antioch without resistance, as well as all the cities in Syria. The only significant resistance encountered by the victorious conquerors was in Palestine. While Jerusalem managed to withstand the siege, the persistent Caliph Umar compelled its inhabitants to surrender the city in 638.

---

[i] Howard-Johnston, *East Rome, Sasanian Persia and the End of Antiquity*.
[ii] Ostrogorsky, *History of the Byzantine State*;
[iii] Howard-Johnston, *East Rome, Sasanian Persia and the End of Antiquity*; Hoyland, *In God's Path*.

After the conquest of Syria, the Arab army continued its advance into Persia and occupied the Byzantine part of Mesopotamia in 639.[i] By the following year, 640, the strongest fortress in Armenia, Dvin, surrendered. Thus, all Byzantine territories east of the Mediterranean fell under Muslim control in less than ten years. The fate of Egypt remained uncertain.

While Emperor Heraclius (r. 610-641) personally led the empire's successful campaign against the Sasanian Persians, his involvement in the struggle against the emerging Arab Muslim forces was far less direct. Initially, he attempted to oversee military operations from Antioch, but after the catastrophic defeat at Yarmouk, he lost all hope. Before his eyes, his life's accomplishments had fallen away, and as it turned out, his heroic victory against Persia was futile. All the Byzantine Christian lands he had liberated from the Persians were lost with the advent of the new religion, against which no one had the strength to resist.[ii] This physically and mentally broke the old emperor to the extent that he could no longer endure sea voyages.

In addition to the defeat at Yarmouk, matters became even more tragic in Constantinople. Political struggles over the issue of succession began with the ailing Emperor Heraclius, who died on February 11th, 641, from illness. After Heraclius died, unrest engulfed the empire, which divided itself in support of his sons. In his will, Emperor Heraclius designated his sons Constantine III and Heraclonas to rule jointly as co-emperors, with Martina—Heraclonas's mother—acting in a supervisory role. His eldest son from his first marriage, Constantine III, briefly ruled but died of tuberculosis.[iii] His death was exploited by Heraclius's younger son from his second marriage, Heraclonas, who, along with his mother Martina, seized the crown. Martina supported Monothelite teachings and restored the exiled Pyrrhus to the position of patriarch (the religious leader of the Byzantine Church), who, in turn, appointed the zealous Monothelite Cyrus as bishop of Alexandria. This caused significant religious unrest in Constantinople and great opposition against the emperor and his mother.[iv]

---

[i] Kennedy, *The Great Arab Conquests*.
[ii] Hoyland, *In God's Path*.
[iii] Ostrogorsky, *History of the Byzantine State*.
[iv] Ibid.

# The Threat Rises

The new government in Constantinople considered further resistance against the Arab invasion futile and ordered Bishop Cyrus to negotiate with the Muslims in Alexandria. Cyrus concluded a peace treaty in which virtually all of Egypt was surrendered to the conquerors. Dissatisfaction with these decisions spilled over to the troops in Asia Minor, which supported the population of Constantinople and deposed the hated Heraclonas, Martina, and Pyrrhus from power.

After the old ruler's exile to Rhodes, the Senate chose the ten-year-old son of Constantine III, Constans II (r. 641-668), as the new emperor.[i] The new emperor, under the tutelage of the strengthened Senate, had to fulfill the signed agreement to surrender Alexandria to Patriarch Cyrus and the Arabs. Byzantine troops left Alexandria on September 12$^{th}$, 642, embarking for Rhodes. The Arab commander Amr ibn Kulthum entered the city and extended his authority along the North African coast to Tripoli.[ii] The new caliph, Uthman (r. 644-656), recalled Amr ibn Kulthum with his army from Alexandria due to obligations in the east, which emboldened the Byzantines to launch an offensive. A strong fleet from Constantinople, under the command of Manuel, disembarked in Alexandria and captured the city by surprise. However, this victory was short-lived, as Amr ibn Kulthum besieged and recaptured Alexandria in 646. Manuel left Egypt with his garrison, while the Coptic population, along with their Monothelite patriarch, submitted to the Arabs. This act marked Byzantium's permanent loss of its richest and economically strongest province.

From Egypt, the Arab forces continued their advance westward toward the Exarchate of Carthage, where Exarch Gregory the Patrician had proclaimed himself emperor in defiance of Constantinople.[iii] The usurper Gregory was supported by the local Monophysite population and Moorish tribes. Exploiting the revolt, the Arabs sacked the usurper's residence in Sufetula in 647 and killed Gregory, after which they received a large tribute from the legitimate authorities to withdraw to Egypt.

The territories of the Byzantine Empire in the remaining part of Armenia, as well as Anatolia itself, were threatened by the governor of

---

[i] Bury, *A History of the Later Roman Empire*.
[ii] Kennedy, *The Great Arab Conquests*.
[iii] Hoyland, *In God's Path*.

Syria, the capable military leader Muawiyah. In 642 and 643, Muawiyah launched a major incursion into Armenia, besieging fortresses with the aim of cutting off Constantinople. Amassing large contingents of troops, in 647, he penetrated into Cappadocia, capturing Caesarea before advancing into Phrygia. While plundering the wealthy province, he failed to take the heavily fortified city of Amorium. However, his return to Damascus was crowned with rich spoils and numerous captives.

Muawiyah's military genius is evidenced by the fact that he was the first statesman to recognize that the struggle against Byzantium was impossible without a strong fleet.[i] The governorship of Syria and access to the Mediterranean enabled Muawiyah to redirect resources that had been acquired through conquests into building the first Arab fleet. However, he did not have the support of Caliph Umar in this endeavor. Circumstances changed after Umar's death when Caliph Uthman assumed power and lent support to Muawiyah's plan.[ii]

Muawiyah.[17]

Personally leading the first Islamic fleet he created, Muawiyah attacked Cyprus in 649 and captured the capital, Salamis (Constantia). After signing a three-year truce with Byzantium, Muawiyah used the respite to build an even larger and better fleet. In 654, the Arabs devastated Rhodes, carrying off the famous Colossus of Rhodes to their territory. Crete and several Cycladic and Sporadic islands were also ravaged. Following these attacks, Kos, Rhodes, and Cyprus remained in Arab possession. There is no doubt that Muawiyah's primary goal was Constantinople even then. This was clear to the emperor and those around him, prompting them to

---

[i] Nicolle, *The Great Islamic Conquests, AD 632-750*.
[ii] Hoyland, *In God's Path*.

assemble a strong fleet near the Anatolian coast to confront Muawiyah. Emperor Constans II (r. 641-668) personally led the fleet in the naval battle of 655, which also happened to be the first Arab-Byzantine battle. It ended in catastrophe for the Byzantines, with the emperor narrowly escaping death.

Further major offensives against Byzantium were averted by the civil war in the Rashidun Caliphate, which followed the assassination of Caliph Uthman in 656. The First Fitna, a prolonged civil war between the two proclaimed caliphs, Ali and Muawiyah, lasted until 661 and provided temporary relief for Byzantium.[i]

In the last five years of his life, Emperor Constans II spent his time in Italy and Sicily, relinquishing his involvement in Eastern politics due to the seemingly hopeless situation. He was assassinated in 668 in Syracuse in a palace conspiracy led by close associates of the court. The usurpers proclaimed one of their own, Mezezius, as the new emperor, but he was killed by the army of the Ravenna Exarchate, which quelled the uprising in 669.[ii] Upon the emperor's assassination, his young son, Constantine IV (r. 668-685), ascended to the throne, injecting new energy into the Byzantine-Arab conflicts.

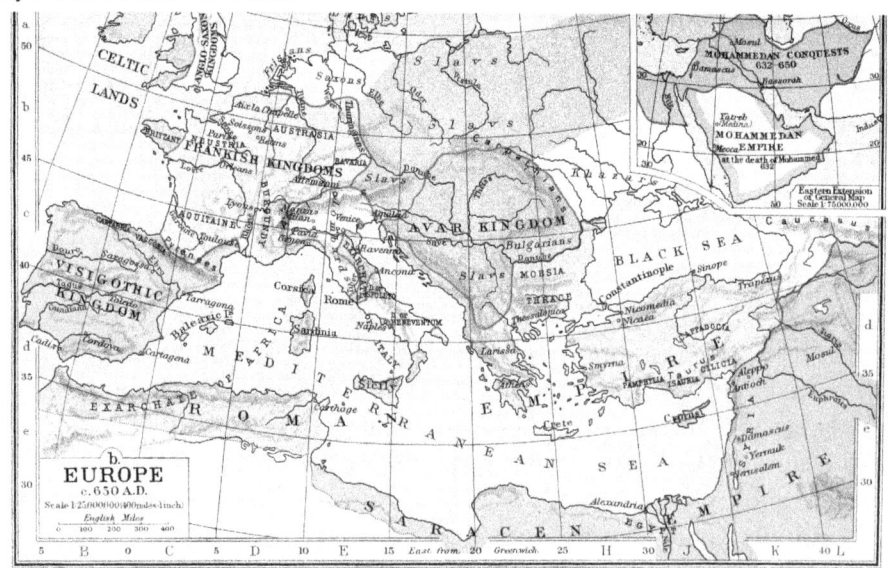

Europe in the mid-7th century.[18]

---

[i] Nicolle, *The Great Islamic Conquests, AD 632-750*.
[ii] Ostrogorsky, *History of the Byzantine State*.

# The Umayyad Caliphate

Muawiyah I (r. 661-680) achieved victory in the First Fitna after a five-year struggle. He founded the Umayyad Caliphate and transferred the state's center to Damascus. By winning the civil war, Muawiyah introduced the rule that succession to the throne was heredity rather than by election, as was the case in the Rashidun Caliphate.

After pacifying the situation in the caliphate in 663, the Arabs renewed their struggle against Byzantium. Their raids became more frequent, and each year was marked by Arab devastation for the next fifteen years.[i] Their incursions reached as far as Chalcedon on the Bosphorus, where some units spent the winter and continued to ravage the once-rich Byzantine Anatolian provinces. The Arabs briefly occupied the island of Chios in 670, and one of Muawiyah's commanders managed to conquer the Peninsula of Cyzicus, located in the immediate vicinity of Constantinople.[ii] This created a solid base for an attack on Constantinople, which Muawiyah had long coveted.

Before the attack, his fleet secured complete control of the Lycian and Cilician coasts, as well as the conquest of Smyrna in 672, giving him complete control of the rear. In the spring of 674, the main action of the attack on Constantinople began. The city was initially besieged by sea with a large Arab fleet, which was supported by infantry advancing from Cyzicus. The battles lasted throughout the summer, with the Muslim fleet withdrawing to Cyzicus in the autumn. The next spring, the fleet reappeared and once again besieged Constantinople throughout the summer, a pattern that repeated in the following years. Constantinople, as the largest fortress of the time, could not be conquered, and due to their great losses, the Arabs were forced to abandon the naval siege in 678.[iii] The Arabs suffered heavy losses in battles under the walls of Constantinople because of the Byzantine use of Greek fire, which was first mentioned in contemporary sources during this siege.

Greek fire was an invention of the architect Callinicus from Syria. It was an explosive material composed of saltpeter, the ingredients of which were known exclusively to the Byzantines. Using siphons mounted on ships, Greek fire was thrown onto enemy vessels, causing intense fires. It

---

[i] Nicolle, *The Great Islamic Conquests, AD 632-750*.
[ii] Ibid
[iii] Kennedy, *The Great Arab Conquests*.

was first used in the Arab siege of Constantinople (674-678) and, from then on, frequently served in offensive and defensive actions, ensuring the Byzantines' technological superiority over surrounding enemies.

The Umayyad Caliphate at the height of its power in the early 8th century CE.[19]

Muawiyah's fleet suffered losses in a storm that struck near the Pamphylian coast (a region in the south of Asia Minor), and simultaneously, the Arab army was defeated in Asia Minor.[i] All of this forced Caliph Muawiyah I to negotiate a peace treaty with Byzantium for thirty years with an annual payment of tribute. As the historian Theophanes notes in his work, "And great peace reigned in the East and in the West." The unsuccessful long siege of Constantinople resonated far beyond the Byzantine Empire's borders and restored the shaken position of the empire.[ii]

---

[i] Nicolle, *The Great Islamic Conquests, AD 632-750*.
[ii] Ostrogorsky, *History of the Byzantine State*.

# The Succession of Constans II

Emperor Constans II was assassinated in 668 while bathing, likely as part of a conspiracy aimed at installing Mezezius, a Byzantine-Armenian general, as emperor. His son, Constantine IV, suppressed the usurpation and assumed the throne. Constantine IV successfully resisted the Arab siege of Constantinople (674-678) and became one of the first emperors to confront the rising Bulgarian threat in the Balkans. Despite setbacks in the Danube region, his reign had a lasting impact on Byzantine internal stability and foreign policy. He died around the age of thirty-three in 685 and was succeeded by his sixteen-year-old son, Justinian II (r. 685-695, 705-711), a capable but autocratic ruler. Thanks to his father's victory over the Arabs, Justinian enjoyed peace in the East during the early part of his reign.

After the death of Muawiyah I, the caliphate fell into an internal crisis until the next caliph, Abd al-Malik (r. 685-711), consolidated power and signed a new treaty with Byzantium. This treaty was more favorable than the previous one, as it brought the emperor a larger annual tribute along with the division of revenues from Armenia, Iberia, and Cyprus.[i]

Encouraged by his successes against the Slavs in the Balkans, Justinian II continued the policy of resettlement throughout the empire. He resettled a large part of the population of Cyprus to the devastated Cyzicus, refusing to inform the caliphate about it. Disregarding the caliph's protests, Justinian II reignited hostilities with Muslim forces around 691. In 692, at the Battle of Sebastopolis, he suffered a major defeat, partly due to the defection of Slavic troops that switched sides at a critical moment. As a result of this loss, Justinian was forced to sign a treaty that ceded tax revenues and influence in Armenia and Iberia to the Umayyads.

New problems for Byzantium were caused by a revolt against Justinian II in 695, which the Arabs knew how to exploit. The turmoil that followed paralyzed defensive operations in distant parts of the empire for the next twenty years. The Arabs broke through in 697 and captured Carthage, prompting Emperor Leontius (r. 695-698) to send a fleet to restore the Exarchate of Carthage. The fleet managed to regain the city briefly, but by the following spring, the Arab fleet had forced the Byzantines to permanently abandon their North African territories.

---

[i] Hoyland, *In God's Path*.

The new emperor, Tiberius III (r. 698-705), did not even attempt to restore the Exarchate of Carthage, so no one slowed down Arab advances until Ceuta, where the last Byzantine garrison was located.[i] With the fall of Ceuta in 711, the caliphate seized control of the entire coast of North Africa and reached the Atlantic Ocean. This would be the starting point for the fateful crossing of Arab commander Tariq ibn Ziyad into Europe in 711.[ii] He took a detour through Africa since the strong walls of Constantinople prevented a direct route from the east.

From the eastern front, the Arabs continued to exploit the unrest in the Byzantine Empire, and in 709, they besieged the fortress of Tyana, where they dealt a heavy blow to the Byzantines. This defeat again broke the Byzantine defense system and led to Arab raids in Cilicia in 710 and 711. Emperor Anastasius II (r. 713-715) attempted to counterattack to suppress the attacks, but it failed due to internal crises. Once again, the fate of Byzantium was decided under the walls of Constantinople. In August 717, Constantinople was besieged for the second time by both land and sea, just like forty years prior. This time, the Byzantines managed to destroy the enemy fleet with Greek fire while the walls withstood the Arab assaults. Furthermore, the winter of 717-18 was unusually cold, causing famine, epidemics, and deaths among the Muslim forces. The decisive contribution to a victory was made by twenty thousand Bulgarian cavalry troops led by Khan Tervel, an old ally of Emperor Justinian II, who inflicted heavy losses on the Arabs. Due to significant losses, on August 15$^{th}$, 718, the Arab ships left the waters of Constantinople, thus ending another siege of Constantinople.[iii]

After another unsuccessful attempt to conquer Constantinople, the Arabs consolidated their troops and again threatened Asia Minor in 726 by capturing Caesarea and besieging Nicaea. The end of Byzantine troubles in regards to their territory would be resolved by Emperor Leo III the Isaurian (r. 717-741) with a great victory at Akroinon in 740 and his alliance with the Khazars to reduce the major incursions of the Arabs.[iv]

With the liberation of Constantinople and Asia Minor from the Arabs, an important stage in the Byzantine-Arab struggle came to an end. Constantinople would no longer experience any siege by the Arabs in the

---

[i] Ostrogorsky, *History of the Byzantine State*.
[ii] Nicolle, *The Great Islamic Conquests, AD 632-750*.
[iii] Ibid.
[iv] Diehl, *History of the Byzantine Empire*.

future, ensuring the survival of the Byzantine Empire. Just as in 678, when Constantine IV halted the Arab invasion for the first time with the defense of Constantinople, Leo III's victory in 718, like the success of Charles Martel at Poitiers in 732, determined the fate of Europe. Constantinople was the last barrier standing in the way of a Muslim invasion, and the city's survival was not only a salvation for the Byzantine Empire but also for European culture and civilization.

# Chapter 7: Iconoclasm

**Introduction**

The Byzantine Empire at the end of the 7$^{th}$ century was shaken by military, internal, religious, and even natural crises. The combination of these dangers and geopolitical realities required a different climate in the Eastern Roman Empire. It was trying to find an outlook that would make peace in the state, security in the region, and renew the relationship with the divine. Iconoclasm was the manifestation of the latter, but it was caused by all of the mentioned factors.[i]

The 7$^{th}$ century was particularly hard, and Byzantium saw a decrease in its geopolitical significance. In 602, the Eastern Roman Empire fought for the domination of the Middle East with the Persian Sasanian Empire. The Sasanian army won Armenia, Syria, Palestine, and Egypt. A few years later, the Sasanian army was camping outside of Constantinople.[ii]

In the end, this political crisis was successfully managed by the Byzantine Empire, but the most significant effect of these wars was the neglect of the events unfolding in the Arabian Peninsula by both empires. At this time, Muhammad was going from Mecca to Medina, spreading the seed of a new religion. Just a decade later, the followers of the new religion would control the whole Arabian Peninsula, forming the Rashidun Caliphate, which started after the death of Prophet Muhammad in 632 and ended with the internal conflict of 661.

---

[i] Brubaker and Haldon, *Byzantium in the Iconoclast Era (ca. 680-850)*.
[ii] Howard-Johnston, *East Rome, Sasanian Persia and the End of Antiquity*.

During this period, the Arabs saw the conquest of both Byzantine and Persian territory. The Byzantines lost all the territory they regained from the Sasanians, including Egypt, Palestine, and the Caucasus, thus losing undisputed control of the Mediterranean. The Persian Empire had suffered dire consequences and was consumed by the Arab conquest.[i]

The 7th century saw the demise of the Heraclian dynasty, which ended with internal instability. The Twenty Years' Anarchy is a term used for the period of internal instability in the Byzantine Empire. This period saw the rapid succession of several emperors to the throne between the first deposition of Justinian II in 695 and the ascent of Leo III the Isaurian to the throne in 717, marking the beginning of the Isaurian dynasty.[ii]

The Byzantine Empire in the early 8th century.[20]

Leo III (r. 717-741) successfully ended the period of military coups and instability, but the state he inherited was much weaker than it had been a century earlier. The hegemony of the Mediterranean ended, with the Levant and North Africa being under Arab control, the Balkans being attacked by the Bulgars, and lost influence over Italy and the papacy to the growing power of the Franks. His rule also marked the beginning of the First Iconoclasm, which occurred between 726 and 787.

Iconoclasm is the deliberate destruction of a culture's religious images and other symbols or monuments, usually for religious or political motives (from Greek εἰκών or *eikṓn*, "figure" or "icon" and κλάω or *kláō*, "to break"). Conversely, people who revere or venerate religious images are

---

[i] Nicolle, *The Great Islamic Conquests, AD 632-750*.
[ii] Bury, *A History of the Later Roman Empire*.

derisively called "iconolaters" (εἰκονολάτρες).[i] They are normally known as "iconodules" (εἰκονόδουλοι) or "iconophiles" (εἰκονόφιλοι). These terms were, however, not a part of the Byzantine debate over images; rather, they have been brought into common usage by modern historians. The Byzantine term for the debate over religious imagery was iconomachy, meaning "struggle over images." The breaking of the icons was an attempt to stop the already established practice of depicting Jesus, Mary, and the saints through canonized imagery. So, if that tradition already existed, what caused the controversy and change of heart?

First of all, the Arab conquests didn't only change the eastern borders of the Byzantine Empire; they also brought some old ideas about the depiction of God. Judaism, as the first Abrahamic religion, had a strict understanding of God as the impersonal and omnipotent. God was a universal force beyond human comprehension. As such, depictions of God were strictly forbidden, and any attempt at a physical representation of God was seen as blasphemous and idol worship. We can find that directly in the Old Testament in Exodus 20:4: "You shall not make for yourself a carved image, or any likeness of anything that is in heaven above, or that is in the earth beneath, or that is in the water under the earth," thus forbidding any depiction of God.

However, with Christ understood as God in the flesh, with his human and divine nature coexisting, the Christians argued that God intentionally came closer to humanity by becoming flesh. This is confirmed in the New Testament in Colossians 1:15: "The Son is the image of the invisible God, the firstborn over all creation." Thus, the veneration of icons was not understood as idol worship since they were a means of worship, not the object of worship.

Islam brought the idea of iconoclasm back into the spotlight. Muslims have a very strict policy on not depicting God in any shape or form. This is extended to prophets, such as Muhammad and Jesus, who are understood to be prophets in Islam. With the expansion of Islam, this view was reintroduced to the Byzantines.[ii]

What is important to understand is that theological dilemmas were taken very seriously in this period. Religion had roles that are today being done by science, art, and politics. In other words, Christianity explained

---

[i] Kolrud and Prusac, *Iconoclasm from Antiquity to Modernity*.
[ii] Ibid.

that "God's will" manifested in military and political successes. In other words, military losses and political crises were observed as a way of God correcting the path of an empire.

With the loss of territory and power in the region, the Byzantines observed the rise of Islam. The Eastern Roman Empire was also stricken by the volcanic eruption of Santorini, which was paired with external and internal political crises. These were all seen as a sign from God that something was wrong with Christian devotion.

## The First Iconoclast Era

Another reason that might explain the introduction of iconoclasm by Leo III is his Syrian roots. The Byzantine Empire had two roots: Western, which was more Roman or Greek, and Eastern, which was associated more with the Levant and closer to ideas of Islam. Leo was the first ruler of the first non-Greek or Roman dynasty, which might have affected him to search for spiritual rebranding in Eastern traditions.

An icon of Mary, the mother of Jesus, 6ᵗʰ century.[21]

Leo's stance against religious images became evident when he ordered the removal of a particularly revered icon of Christ from the imperial palace in 725.[i] This symbolic act marked the beginning of a movement that would soon engulf the empire. The situation further culminated in the official ban on icons, which happened in 730.

Leo's iconoclastic policies drew condemnation from Pope Gregory II in Rome, sparking a rift between the Eastern and Western branches of Christianity. The pope vehemently opposed Leo's ban on icons, which culminated in the pope's declaration of iconoclasm as heretical that same year, further exacerbating tensions between the Byzantine Empire and the papacy.

The iconoclastic fervor continued after Leo's death under Constantine V (r. 741-775, who enforced his father's policies with even greater zeal).[ii] The biggest difference is that Constantine persecuted the people who didn't follow the iconoclastic policies with an extensive purge of the military and bureaucracy of icon worshipers. His father, on the contrary, only destroyed the icons.

The reign of Constantine V also witnessed the rise of the iconophile movement, which was led by those who vehemently opposed the destruction of religious images. This culminated in the revolt of iconophiles in 750, which challenged the authority of the emperor and iconoclastic ideology.

The last years of Constantine's reign were also unsuccessful politically. In 751, the Byzantines lost the northern Italian territories for good. The Exarchate of Ravenna was lost to the Lombards, which caused the pope to turn away from the Byzantine Empire even more. Not only were Eastern Roman heretics ignoring the supposedly higher status of the pope, but they were also proving less and less useful as potential allies. They couldn't guarantee the safety of the pope, but the Franks could. The Franks also recognized the pope's superior authority in church matters. This territorial decline further weakened the empire's position on the international stage and strained its relations with neighboring powers.

Constantine V was succeeded by his young son Leo IV, who took full rule in 775.[iii] He died only five years later, in 780. His

---

[i] Besançon, *The Forbidden Image*.
[ii] Ostrogorsky, *History of the Byzantine State*.
[iii] Ibid.

politics were not too influential on the matter of iconoclasm. He agreed with his father, but he did stop the oppression of iconophiles. What is important is that he left the throne to his wife since his son, Constantine VI, was only nine years old at the time. Leo's wife and *de facto* ruler and regent for her son Constantine VI was called Irene, also known as Irene of Athens, and she was the first iconophile ruler after the establishment of the Isaurian dynasty.[i] She wasn't just sympathetic to the icons; she made it her mission to abolish iconoclasm with vigor, intelligence, and ruthlessness.

That was an extremely difficult task, as previous emperors had eradicated support for icons not only from the church hierarchy but also from public life and the army. Irene's first step was to install someone she trusted as the patriarch of Constantinople. However, the church had been purged of iconophile sympathizers. She appointed her trusted secretary, Tarasios, to the position. Although a layman at the time, Irene used her influence at court to fast-track his ordination, allowing him to assume the patriarchate and assist in restoring the veneration of icons.

This raised tensions in the empire, but Irene didn't stop there. In 786, she attempted to condemn iconoclasm as an official heresy at a church council held at the Church of the Holy Apostles in Constantinople. However, iconoclast troops in the imperial army revolted, preventing the council from proceeding. To deal with this opposition, Irene acted strategically: she dispatched the iconoclast elements of the army on a military campaign to Asia Minor, only to inform them upon arrival that they were dismissed from service. With the opposition removed, she convened a new council the following year.

In 787, Irene organized the Seventh Ecumenical Council, also known as the Second Council of Nicaea, which officially condemned iconoclasm and reaffirmed the veneration of religious images within the Byzantine Empire. This council marked the end of the first iconoclast crisis.[ii]

There was also a chance for possibly mending the rift between East and West, not only by condemning iconoclasm and affirming the legitimacy of icon veneration but also with the proposal of marriage between King Charlemagne of the Franks and Irene of Athens. However, this didn't happen. Irene turned out to be the last ruler of the Isaurian dynasty. In

---

[i] Bury, *A History of the Later Roman Empire*.
[ii] Bury.

797, she—or her supporters—had her son Constantine VI blinded and deposed seven years after he had assumed full imperial authority. Although Constantine became the sole emperor in 790, Irene never ceased to exert considerable influence over imperial policy. Eventually, her supporters conspired to remove him and consolidate her rule. The ruthless court politics and intrigues of Irene's regime made her deeply unpopular, leading to her overthrow in 802 by Nikephoros, her finance minister.[i]

The rule of Nikephoros tried to move from the iconophile versus iconoclast rift, leaving the official dogma as Irene had put it. At that moment, there were still iconoclast supporters but also iconophiles who wanted the persecution of the iconoclasts. However, this situation didn't last. Nikephoros was focused on tax revisions and the new military campaign in the Balkans against the Bulgars. He died in conquest against Krum the Bulgar in 811; his army was decimated after a previously successful campaign. The crown was inherited by his son-in-law, Michael I Rangabe (r. 811-813), who managed to flee from the battlefield back to Constantinople.[ii] His reign was short since he was quickly overthrown by the strategos Leo, who crowned himself as Leo V the Armenian (r. 813-820). The rule of Leo V also marked the second and last iconoclast era, which lasted from 814 to 842.[iii]

## The Second Iconoclast Era

Under Leo V, iconoclasm was reinstated, reflecting the enduring popularity of the movement among certain segments of Byzantine society. The sentiment was similar to before the First Iconoclast crisis. The country was going through a difficult time, with the military failures of the Bulgars in the north and the Abbasid Caliphate in the south, which was going through its golden age.[iv] Yet again, this was interpreted as the consequence of icon worship by Emperor Leo V and his advisors, and they started policies to purify the church of icons and persecute iconophiles.

---

[i] Ostrogorsky, *History of the Byzantine State*.
[ii] Ibid
[iii] Ibid.
[iv] Hoyland, *In God's Path*.

Depiction of Leo V.[22]

The policies of iconophile tolerance were briefly reinstated with Michael II the Amorion (also called the Stammerer), who overturned Leo V in 820. As a ruler, Michael II had a lot of crises to attend to. His conquest of the throne was organized by his followers since he was imprisoned and sentenced to execution by Leo V. In a last-ditch attempt, his followers killed Leo V in church on Christmas Eve in 820, thus starting Michael's reign, which lasted until 829. He had a turbulent and challenging rule with potential usurpers of the throne, such as Thomas the Slav, who represented himself as Constantine VI, the blinded son of Irene. This attempt led to a siege of Constantinople in 823, which was unsuccessful due to the arrival of the Bulgars from the west.

The last thing that Michael II wanted was more problems, so he tried to make peace between iconophiles and iconoclasts by forbidding the discussion of the issue. However, both iconophile zealots and iconoclasts tried to push their cause during this period. For example, iconophile zealots cooperated with the pope in pushing for the full return of icons and a complete ban on iconoclast heresy. As a consequence, the pope sent a convoy to appeal to Michael, but he didn't appreciate this attempt to meddle in his rule, so he imprisoned them for a while, thus dividing Byzantine and Rome even more.

The successor of Michael II was his son Theophilus (r. 829-842), the last iconoclast emperor.[i] The young emperor was a well-educated iconoclast, similar to Constantine V, who was a great admirer of Arab culture. Furthermore, he was a close friend of John the Grammarian, who was one of the most accomplished iconoclast scholars. Apart from being a friend and a mentor to Theophilus, he was also appointed patriarch in 837 by the blessing of the emperor.

This period witnessed the peak of the second iconoclast persecution, which saw emperors and royalists clashing with iconophile zealots. The death of Theophilus in 842 marked the end of the iconoclast persecution. Theophilus left a young son and a very capable iconophile wife in charge of the throne.

The mother of the young emperor Michael III and his regent was Theodora, who brought the end of iconoclasm to Byzantium.[ii] Her reign was a mixture of favorable geopolitical occurrences and well-executed political moves, especially when it came to defeating the iconoclasts. First, the military conquest of Sicily and southern Italy by the Aghlabid Emirate served as evidence that the military downfall of the Eastern Roman Empire was not because of the icons. Additionally, Theodora spread the rumor that Theophilus had repented for persecuting the iconophiles on his deathbed, which served as additional proof. All of these circumstances allowed her to align herself with the zealot party and replace John the Grammarian with an iconophile patriarch, which ended the iconoclast episode. Her politics were further enforced by her son Michael III, which cemented the future of iconoclasm as a fringe movement out of the spotlight of Byzantine politics.[iii]

## The Consequences of Iconoclasm

The iconoclastic controversy was interpreted by scholars as the Byzantine Empire choosing between Western and Eastern traditions. Though this is a very sound explanation, the iconoclastic movement also represents the adjustment to the new geopolitical reality that saw the fall of some important empires, such as Persia, and the rise of new ones, such as the Muslim caliphates. Even though it was a sort of adjustment phase, it also provoked a serious chain of events. For example, it strained the

---

[i] Ostrogorsky, *History of the Byzantine State*.
[ii] Besançon, *The Forbidden Image*.
[iii] Ibid.

relationship between the Eastern and Western branches of the Christian Church, particularly between the pope and the Byzantine Empire. The divergent views on the use of religious images deepened the schism between the two churches, leaving a lasting impact on the religious landscape of Europe.[i]

In conclusion, the Byzantine iconoclasm era was a complex and tumultuous period in the history of the Byzantine Empire and was characterized by religious fervor, political intrigue, and cultural upheaval. Spanning over a century, this conflict left a profound impact on Byzantine society and its relationship with the wider Christian world. Despite its eventual resolution, the legacy of the iconoclastic controversy continued to resonate throughout the Byzantine Empire and beyond, shaping the course of religious and political developments for centuries to come.

---

[i] Ibid.

# Part Three: Byzantium's Heyday (867–1025 CE)

# Chapter 8: Christianization of the Slavs

By the 9th century, South Slavs fostered their strongholds in the Balkans and started forming their first states. For centuries, Slavs contributed to the general chaotic state of affairs in the Balkans. We have mentioned previously that Slavs, together with the Avars and Sasanians, attempted to invade Constantinople in the 7th century without success.

The Slavs were a nuisance to the Byzantine Empire, settling in areas that the Byzantines considered their own, engaging in skirmishes, heists, looting, and pillaging. However, South Slavs were there to stay, and they became stronger and stronger. With South Slavic states forming in the Balkans and the Russian state forming in the north, it became clear to the Byzantine emperors that Slavs needed to be placated and pacified somehow. Moreover, if the Byzantines were too slow to exert their cultural influence upon the Slavic peoples, western Europe would most certainly do so, undermining Byzantine influence right at the empire's doorstep. As we will soon see, there was a lot of friction and tension between Western and Eastern Christian missionaries in the Balkans and eastern Europe.

Instead of conquering the Slavs with a sword, the Byzantines conquered Slavs by exerting their culture, most importantly Christianity. For centuries, missionaries from the Byzantine Empire strolled through the Balkans (and farther), bringing enlightenment, literacy, and the monotheistic religion to the Slavs.

The Bulgars, who were among the first to form stable states in the Balkan Peninsula, were also one of the ethnic groups that were influenced the most by the Byzantine Empire. The Bulgars were finally Christianized in the 9th century under their ruler Khan Boris I. After exploring potential ties with western Europe, particularly with King Louis the German, Boris ultimately turned toward Eastern Christianity. Following a military defeat by the Byzantine Empire and ongoing diplomatic pressure, Boris accepted baptism in 864, marking the formal conversion to Christianity.[i] Mass conversion of the Bulgar population began in 865.

The subsequent events are indicative of what typically happens when a country decides to suddenly enforce a completely new religion. Boris faced dissent and bitterness on all fronts. His feudal nobles (boyars) revolted, with the rebellion only subsiding after a number of boyars were executed. Pagan temples were destroyed all around Bulgaria, and the country was flooded by Byzantine preachers. Interestingly, missionaries from other places started to arrive, such as Arab Muslims, contributing to the religious chaos that reigned in the country.[ii]

To make matters even more complicated, Boris started questioning his decision to accept Eastern Christianity. Byzantine Emperor Michael III bluntly refused Boris's demands for the Bulgarian Church's independence, which prompted Boris to turn once again toward the West. Although the talks with Rome turned out to be unsuccessful, the Byzantine Empire, alarmed at the prospect of losing cultural influence over Bulgaria, decided to grant relative religious autonomy to Bulgaria. In 870, the Bulgarian Church obtained the status of archbishopric under the jurisdiction of the Patriarchate of Constantinople.[iii] This was followed by a period of relative religious stability, which saw Bulgaria become a center of Eastern Christianity, helping spread Byzantine cultural influence throughout the Balkans. Bulgaria became a foothold of missionaries, which included Clement, Nahum, and Angelarius, who were disciples of Cyril and Methodius, two important Byzantine missionaries of the period.

There is evidence pointing to a possible early Christianization of Serbs in the Balkan Peninsula, way back in the 7th century.[iv] These efforts were

---

[i] DIMITROV, Ivan Zhelev. Bulgarian Christianity. The Blackwell Companion to Eastern Christianity, 2007, 47.
[ii] Ibid.
[iii] Ibid.
[iv] Ilić, Nikola. *Da li je srpski knez Višeslav bio Hrišćanin?* Teološki Pogledi, 55(1), 95-112

made during Emperor Heraclius's reign, with Roman missionaries arriving in the Balkan Peninsula to Christianize Serbs. However, it seems that these initial efforts, in the case of the Serbs, were not successful or at least not as successful as the later efforts of Emperor Basil I in the 9th century, which saw a large part of the Serbian population adopt Eastern Christianity.

We know quite a bit about both of these Christianization attempts thanks to a later emperor, Constantine VII Porphyrogenitus (r. 913-959), and his manuscript Πρὸς τὸν ἴδιον υἱὸν αὑτοῦ Ῥωμανὸν ("To my son Romanos"), widely known as *On the Governance of the Empire*. The manuscript was essentially a how-to-guide made by Constantine VII for his son Romanos and included a lot of information on ethnic groups deemed important for the politics of the Byzantine Empire.

Constantine VII writes that during the reign of Emperor Basil I (r. 867-886), Croatian and Serbian emissaries came to Constantinople to ask the emperor to dispatch missionaries, who would complete the previous Christianization attempts of the 7th century.[i]

### Preaching in the Language of the Slavs

A major game changer in the Christianization of the Slavs was the strategy taken by Byzantine missionaries. Cyril and Methodius, venerated as saints by all major Christian churches, are today known as the "apostles" of the Slavs.[ii] Cyril (826-869) and Methodius (815-885) were brothers from Greece, spending their early years in Thessalonica, a major city in modern-day northern Greece, northwest of the Chalcidice Peninsula. By that time, the Slavs had already reached deep into the Byzantine Empire, so Cyril and Methodius were able to get acquainted with the language and culture of Slav immigrants fairly early on.

---

[i] Ibid.
[ii] Radic, Radmila. Serbian Christianity. The Blackwell Companion to Eastern Christianity, 2007, 231-248.

Saint Cyril and Methodius.[28]

The father of Cyril and Methodius was a high-ranking military official, and thanks to his influence, the brothers received the best education possible. They weren't simply theologians; they were also intellectuals and able to converse in a number of different languages. This would prove crucial in their efforts to spread the Christian faith among Slavs.

Cyril and Methodius were appointed by Patriarch Photius around 860 as Byzantine missionaries to the Khazars and Slavs. The most significant turning point came with an appeal from Great Moravia (modern-day Czechia and Slovakia) and Prince Rastislav, who, similar to the Bulgarian ruler Boris, vacillated between the East and West and was looking to get the best deal possible. Rastislav was territorially and militarily more under the influence of the West, but he sought to get better terms of cooperation by bringing Eastern preachers into his territory. Perhaps Rastislav wanted to tell the Western rulers that they should offer him better terms or else he would side with the Byzantine Empire.

Whatever the scenario, Cyril and Methodius started developing a new script, the Glagolitic script, in order to transcribe Old Church Slavonic, which is the first standardized literary language of the Slavs. The language was probably in development for some time before Cyril and Methodius standardized it and developed the Glagolitic script to accompany it.

Cyril and Methodius then translated the Bible using Old Church Slavonic and their Glagolitic script. They also developed the Slavic liturgy. Cyril and Methodius were fairly successful in spreading their newly developed script in Great Moravia, but this wasn't always received positively. Cyril and Methodius would encounter missionaries coming from the West, much to the latter's dissatisfaction. Moreover, as they were preaching in Great Moravia, the so-called Photian Schism was reaching its peak.

Patriarch Photius baptizing Bulgarians.[24]

Patriarch Photius, the one who sent Cyril and Methodius on their mission in the first place, ascended to his post in a somewhat dubious fashion. He replaced Patriarch Ignatius, who was probably deposed due to his hostility toward Bardas, a high-ranking noble who managed to become the de facto regent of the young Emperor Michael III after deposing his mother, Theodora. This sort of scenario wasn't really that unusual in Byzantium or Rome. Photius came from an influential family, his uncle being a high-ranking theologian and patriarch in the early $9^{th}$ century. Photius did not meet numerous prerequisites for becoming a patriarch, so he was quickly made into a monk, a deacon, and then a priest. Rome did not accept Photius and regarded him as an illegitimate patriarch. In 863, Pope Nicholas officially condemned Photius and sought to reinstate the old patriarch, Ignatius.

The situation was made even worse by the Bulgarian question that was unraveling at the time. As already mentioned, in the 860s, Bulgarian Khan Boris was deciding whether to accept Eastern or Western influence, finally settling for the East.

In the meantime, debates started to arise over the differences between Latin and Greek Christianity. This threatened to turn into a major schism, especially when Photius condemned Pope Nicholas for heresy, thereby excommunicating the whole Western Church in 867. However, that same year, Basil, the closest advisor to Emperor Michael III, assassinated the emperor. Although he had initially supported Photius, Basil later deposed him and reinstated Ignatius as patriarch, partly to improve relations with the papacy. The assassination marked the end of the Phrygian (Amorian) dynasty and the beginning of the Macedonian dynasty.

This put an end to the Photian Schism, and the two churches gradually rekindled their relationship, although the underlying factors of the schism were never completely removed.

Going back to our main topic, the Christianization of the Slavs, we can now better understand the general context in which Cyril and Methodius operated. They must have had a fairly stressful and challenging job, as they constantly came across other missionaries who ostensibly preached the same faith but served a different master. Cyril and Methodius, however, were fairly well respected in theologian circles and were positively received in Rome in 868. Pope Adrian, who became the next pope after Nicholas, a major antagonist in the Photian Schism, finally granted Cyril and Methodius freedom to continue to spread Christianity with the help of their new script and also accepted the Slavic liturgy. It's possible that Cyril and Methodius, in a way, functioned as a sort of positive mediator between the East and West, helping establish a positive image of the Byzantines among the Roman clergy.

Cyril died in 869, but Methodius continued to preach alone in the regions of Great Moravia and Pannonia. A testament to the still-existing fluidity between the East and West is the fact that Methodius was appointed as archbishop of Pannonia/Moravia by the pope and not by the Constantinople patriarch. He probably resided in Sirmium (modern-day Sremska Mitrovica in Serbia). However, he was quickly captured by Adalwin of Salzburg, Ermanrich of Passau, and Anno of Freising, who considered Methodius a threat to German interests in the region. Methodius was kept in Bavaria.[i]

Thanks to his reputation in Rome, Methodius was quickly released in 873 and got back to spreading the faith. Apparently, he was advised not to use the Slavic liturgy, but he largely ignored this advice. Due to this, animosities with the Western-influenced preachers in Pannonia and Moravia continued, with Methodius having to justify his decisions several more times to authorities in Rome. Methodius finally died in 885. Gorazd, Methodius's student, inherited his position, but he was deposed by the Western clergy. Followers of Cyril and Methodius in Pannonia and Moravia were forced to flee, and they found a new home in Bulgaria, which was much closer to the Byzantine sphere of influence.

### After Cyril and Methodius

This event perhaps shaped the future development of Glagolitsa (the Glagolitic alphabet). In Bulgaria, the disciples of Cyril and Methodius—Clement of Ohrid, Naum of Preslav, and Constantine of Preslav—continued the work of their predecessors, spreading the Eastern version of Christianity, as well as their newly developed alphabet. They formed two schools: the Ohrid Literary School (Ohrid is in modern-day North Macedonia) and the Preslav Literary School. While the Ohrid School was more focused on Glagolitsa, the Preslav School was focused more on the standard Greek alphabet, which culminated in the development of the Cyrillic script. The Cyrillic script of the Preslav School still bore some marks of Glagolitsa but had obvious inclusions from the Greek alphabet. This Cyrillic script completely replaced Glagolitsa and entered into use in

---

[i] Imre, Boba. The Episcopacy of St. Methodius. Slavic Review, 1967, 26.1: 85-93.

numerous countries influenced by the Byzantine Empire. To this day, Serbs, Bulgarians, Macedonians, Montenegrins, and Russians use different variations of the Cyrillic script.

# Chapter 9: The Bulgar Wars

Even though the Bulgarians accepted Eastern Christianity, heralded by the shrewd rule of Boris I, who was able to maintain control over a fairly large area in the Balkan Peninsula, encompassing modern-day Bulgaria, southern Romania, most of Serbia, North Macedonia, and Greece, the situation couldn't remain calm forever.

## A Monk Versus a Wise Man

Boris I abdicated in 889, with his son, Vladimir, inheriting the throne. Vladimir wasn't really like his father; he had other plans for Bulgaria. First of all, it seems that Vladimir didn't care that much about the nascent Bulgarian Christianity and would rather go by the ancient Bulgarian pagan tradition. In fact, Vladimir possibly ordered the destruction of Christian temples and persecuted the clergy. Moreover, he wanted to turn away from the Byzantine Empire altogether and focus more on fostering an alliance with the Germans.[i]

In the meantime, Boris became a monk, hoping to live peacefully in a monastery. However, he had to reclaim the throne and topple his rebellious son Vladimir, who was blinded and removed from political life altogether in 893. Instead of Vladimir, Simeon, Boris's younger son and a monk, was brought to the throne.

---

[i] Leszka, Mirosław J. "The Monk versus the Philosopher: From the History of the Bulgarian-Byzantine War 894–896." *Studia Ceranea* 1 (2011): 55–70.

Therefore, it was up to Simeon, who had received extensive theological education and spent a lot of time in Constantinople, to lead Bulgaria. Simeon was more of an intellectual type and was surrounded by the disciples of Cyril and Methodius. Importantly, he wasn't initially destined for a political or military career; his father wanted Simeon to become the head of the Bulgarian Church. After ascending to the throne, Simeon is said to have remained very humble, steering away from the lush imperial life and choosing to live more like a monk, as he did before.

Emperor Leo VI the Philosopher, son of Emperor Basil, the founder of the Macedonian dynasty, ruled the Byzantine Empire. Much like Simeon, Leo VI was a true intellectual, a wise individual, and active in numerous areas, including theology, legislation, and the military. Also, like Simeon, Leo VI wasn't originally meant to become the emperor; it was only after his older brother Constantine died that Leo had to accept his unexpected promotion to the rank of emperor.

Bulgaria and the Byzantine Empire were led by two very wise gentlemen who weren't really that pretentious or hungry for fame and power. After all, neither of them had much hope of ascending to the throne as they were more steeped in the areas of education and theology.

So, what could go wrong in the relations of these two wise rulers? It is possible that the reasons for the war are purely economic. There's a story about Leo's closest advisor, Basileopator Stylianos Zaoutzes. Zaoutzes had an enslaved eunuch, Musikos, who was connected to Staurakios and Kosmas, two wealthy traders and speculators. They managed to gain approval for several questionable decisions, thanks to their connection with Musikos. First, they raised taxes on Bulgarian goods. Second, they relocated the Bulgarian market within the Byzantine Empire from Constantinople—closer to the source of those goods—to Thessalonica, a city that was both less profitable for Bulgarian merchants and situated along a more dangerous trade route.[i]

---

[i] Ibid.

Emperor Leo VI.[35]

When Simeon complained to Emperor Leo VI, he was rebuffed, the latter receiving reassurance from Stylianos Zaoutzes that everything was going great and that there were no reasons to succumb to the Bulgarian pressure.

### Escalation

That's how the war started between Bulgaria and the Byzantine Empire. The war started in 894 and is known mainly as the Trade War in order to distinguish it from earlier and later conflicts between Bulgarians and Byzantines. Initial military actions were mainly confined to East Thrace, where the Bulgarians were able to defeat the Byzantine expeditionary forces led by Procopius Crenites, who was killed in the battle. Bulgarians allegedly managed to get a hold of a Khazarian regiment, which battled on the side of the Byzantine Empire, proceeding to cut their noses off and sending them back to Constantinople.

Fearing the power of the Bulgarians and angered by what the Bulgarians did to the Khazars, Leo VI managed to convince the Hungarians (or "Turks" as they were referred to back then) to join the war on the Byzantine side. However, the Hungarians had to be ferried across the Danube, which was heavily fenced and blocked by the forces of Simeon, who had received news of the Hungarians' involvement. The Byzantine navy managed to pass the blockade and ferried Hungarians into Bulgaria.

Facing a war on two fronts, south and north, Bulgaria suffered heavy losses, especially from the Hungarians, who managed to penetrate deep into Bulgaria, reaching its biggest cities and plundering and pillaging everything on their way. The Bulgarian army had to seek refuge in fortresses (Hungarians lacked machinery and siege equipment), such as the fortress of Mundraga.

For a little while, it seemed that the war was over and that the Byzantines had won. The year 895 brought more of the same for the Bulgarians, and Simeon once again could do little but sit in a fortress and look as the Hungarians pillaged his lands.

## A Turn of Fate

However, in 895, Simeon managed to regain his composure and inflicted a devastating counterattack on the Hungarians, together with the Pechenegs (the Hungarians' neighbors who were ethnically closely related to them). By the spring of 896, the Bulgarians and Pechenegs had managed to drive the Hungarians out of Bulgaria and forced them to settle farther away in the confines of modern-day Hungary.

Around this time, the Byzantines decided to send another emissary to attempt to negotiate some kind of peace with the Bulgarians. Simeon imprisoned an emissary who had been sent earlier when the situation on the battlefield had been much less favorable to the Bulgarians. Now, Simeon was ready to engage in some kind of dialogue with the current emissary, Leo Choirosphaktes. It is thanks to their correspondence that we know quite a lot about Simeon as a ruler, negotiator, and person. Simeon comes across as fairly straightforward and honest but also a hard negotiator. He would not succumb to Leo's pleas for the release of thousands of Byzantine prisoners in Bulgaria and constantly implicitly mocked the alleged clairvoyant ability of Emperor Leo VI. Simeon, simply put, was trying to get the best deal possible, knowing that the Byzantine Empire didn't have anything else to throw at him. The Hungarians had been defeated, and the Bulgarians repelled the attacks from the Byzantine mainland.

In the summer of 896, Simeon decided to march once again into East Thrace. Emperor Leo VI sent a general to lead the battle instead of him. While previously relying on a very able general, Nikephoros Phokas, Leo VI now turned to Leo Katakalon, the protégé of Stylianos Zaoutzes. It is fairly evident that Zaoutzes had a prominent influence during Leo VI's reign, so much so that he was apparently able to shift public policy and replace high-ranking officials for his own profit.[i] Zaoutzes replaced Nikephoros and bought in Leo Katakalon, a general with lesser merit and experience.

The Bulgarian Empire in the 9th century.[36]

---

[i] Hupchick, P. Dennis, *Simeon's Campaigns for Imperial Recognition, 894-927. The Bulgarian-Byzantine Wars for Early Medieval Balkan Hegemony: Silver-Lined Skulls and Blinded Armies*, 2017, 149-219.

# Bulgarian Victory

The final battle occurred in the vicinity of the village Boulgarophygon ("Bulgar's Bridge"). The battle ended with a decisive Bulgarian victory, and there was more hardship for the Byzantine Empire to come. Katakalon's first officer, Theodosius, was killed in battle, and Katakalon just barely managed to save his own life. The road to Constantinople was open, and Simeon decided to plunder the areas surrounding the Byzantine capital, as he lacked resources for a full-blown siege of Constantinople.

For the time being, in 896, the Bulgarians obtained more favorable trade agreements and forced the Byzantine Empire to pay a hefty tribute. Twenty-five thousand prisoners held by the Bulgarians were handed over to the emperor as part of the agreement.

Taking all of this into consideration, it can be argued that Simeon didn't really obtain that much from the Byzantine Empire; his victory, for the most part, was symbolic. He was recognized as a great leader by the Byzantine Empire, and his supremacy in the Balkans was acknowledged and tolerated, if not accepted. He was also venerated among Bulgarians for his political and military prowess.[i] Simeon developed Preslav into a capital worthy of a great commander. Preslav became the cultural capital of Bulgaria and a major center of the development of Orthodox Christian thought. Simeon, once a humble monk, now proudly wore luxurious symbols of his power:

"...dressed in his gold-woven mantle, wearing a golden necklace, girded with a velvet belt, his shoulders sprinkled with pearls, girded with a golden sword ... with bracelets on his arms, his boyars adorned with golden necklaces, belts, and bracelets."[ii]

The peace between the Bulgars and the Byzantines was marked by countless small Bulgarian expansions at the expense of the Byzantine Empire. The matter was made worse by the Arab expansion. Arabs took over Sicily completely in 902, launching numerous small attacks on the Byzantine coastline. Leo of Tripoli, a Greek captured in Attaleia (modern-day Antalya in Turkey), led numerous devastating attacks on Byzantine coastal towns, the most devastating being the sack of Thessalonica in 904.

---

[i] Ibid.
[ii] Ibid. 165

Leo was once a slave, and he rose to the rank of naval commander and governed Tripoli (modern-day Lebanon), from where numerous Arab raids were launched. Leo Tripolites took advantage of the weak defensive systems of Thessalonica, capturing it and wreaking havoc among the local population.

Simeon, in turn, took advantage of the Thessalonica raid and launched operations in Macedonia. Gathering Slavs along the way, who inhabited the province of Macedonia in great numbers, the Bulgarians threatened Thessalonica, which had already been weakened by the Arab raid. Once again, Leo Choirosphaktes, who had spent years negotiating with the Bulgarians on behalf of Emperor Leo VI, brokered a deal that at least temporarily halted the Bulgarian invasion. However, Bulgaria was not the only threat Byzantium faced.

## The Varangians Versus Byzantines

The Varangians were Viking conquerors who founded Kievan Rus'. They started the Rurik dynasty and eventually assimilated with the surrounding and much more numerous Slavic population, whom they dominated in a sort of feudal system. The Ruriks were the aristocrats (and possibly the most able and best-equipped soldiers), and the Slavs were peasants and servants.

The Ruriks attacked the Byzantine Empire in 830 and 860. It is likely that the reasons for these conflicts were mostly economic, with the Ruriks aiming to inflict swift defeats and get as much goods and money as possible before leaving. In 907, the Ruriks, led by Oleg of Novgorod, sought better trade terms and effectively coerced the Byzantines into paying them to leave the empire in peace, though this peace would, of course, prove temporary.

There are scant reports about the Ruriks invading the Byzantines or returning home from their bountiful Byzantine exploits. What we have is preserved in the *Primary Chronicle* (*Tale of Bygone Years*), one of the oldest Russian written pieces (it was written in the 12$^{th}$ century by Nestor).[i] "Oleg went to the Greeks ... and came Oleg to Kiev taking gold and silks, and vegetables, and wines."[ii]

---

[i] Rukavishnikov, Alexandr. "Tale of Bygone Years: the Russian Primary Chronicle as a family chronicle." Early Medieval Europe 12, no. 1 (2003): 53-74.
[ii] Ibid. p. 66

A modern painting of Oleg, the leader of the Varangians.[27]

The conquest was incredibly bloody:

"They waged war around the city, and accomplished much slaughter of the Greeks. They also destroyed many palaces and burned the churches. Of the prisoners they captured, some they beheaded, some they tortured, some they shot, and still others they cast into the sea. The Russes inflicted many other woes upon the Greeks after the usual manner of soldiers. Oleg commanded his warriors to make wheels which they attached to the ships, and when the wind was favorable, they spread the sails and bore down upon the city from the open country. When the Greeks beheld this, they were afraid, and sending messengers to Oleg, they implored him not to destroy the city and offered to submit to such tribute as he should desire. Thus Oleg halted his troops."[i]

Therefore, it isn't surprising that the Byzantines ultimately decided to pay off the Ruriks and give them what they wanted. The 12th-century Russian chronicler Nestor recorded some of the peace terms between the Ruriks and Byzantines:

---

[i] Nestor. Primary Chronicle. P. 64. https://www.mgh-bibliothek.de/dokumente/a/a011458.pdf

1. The Greeks would pay a hefty tribute directly to the Ruriks who conquered them.
2. The Ruriks would receive as much grain as they wished.
3. They would receive six months' worth of bread, wine, fish, meat, and fruit.
4. Baths (yes, baths) would be prepared by the Greeks for the Ruriks.
5. The Ruriks could engage in tax-free business with the Greeks.
6. The Ruriks should not inflict violence on the Greeks.
7. The Rus' who came to Constantinople would be required to apply to a sort of Rus' consulate in Saint Mamas district in Constantinople so that they could get their monthly allowance.

# Chapter 10: Basil II: The Bulgars' Demise

## Continuation of Conflicts between Bulgaria and Byzantium

In the early 10th century, Byzantium had a lot of internal problems. Emperor Leo VI was desperate for a male heir, and finally, one of his mistresses, Zoë Karbonopsina (Karbonopsina means "coal black eyes"), gave birth to his first male child, Constantine VII. After marrying Zoë, Emperor Leo VI had four marriages under his belt, which didn't really sit well with the religious authorities. This contributed to a rift between religious and political authority in Byzantium.

Leo the Wise died in 912, leaving the empire to Constantine VII, who was only seven years old at the time. Alexander, Leo's brother, was supposed to act as Constantine's co-ruler, but he quickly gathered all the power in his hands, allying with people previously hostile to his brother Leo. Alexander seemed to have been less wise than Leo, as he failed to acknowledge the importance of the Bulgarian threat. Alexander refused to honor the peace agreements made between Leo and Simeon. Even worse, he insulted the Bulgarian delegation, which came to express their condolences over the death of Leo VI, treating them in a despicable and condescending way.

Simeon harbored hopes of becoming the head of a joint Bulgarian-Byzantine Empire, so he launched a new war against Byzantium.

# Campaign after Campaign

Emboldened by his successful wars against the Byzantine Empire, Simeon started to nurture hopes of much larger exploits. In 913, Simeon marched into the Byzantine Empire once again, this time in an even more powerful and dominant fashion. During the conflict that lasted from 894 to 896, the Byzantine Empire was led by a wise and able emperor, Leo VI. In 913, it was nominally led by Constantine VII, Leo's son, who was only around eight years old at the time: his co-ruler, Alexander, died that same year. There was a battle of intrigue, gossip, and political wit in Byzantium. Alexander appointed Patriarch Nicholas Mystikos as Constantine's regent. Mystikos, in turn, feared Zoë, who had been exiled by Alexander, as Mystikos was a bitter opponent of the marriage between Zoë and Leo VI. Mystikos, as if wanting to completely shatter the empire's military organization, ordered the execution of Constantine Doukas, the supreme commander of Byzantium's military.

Simeon found little resistance on his way to Constantinople. The Byzantines, led by Patriarch Mystikos, hurriedly accepted the Bulgarians' terms. Mystikos even ceremonially crowned Simeon, acknowledging him as the emperor of the Bulgarians in 913. Simeon managed to get another concession. One of his daughters would be married to Constantine VII. While this temporarily averted the Bulgarian threat, it came at the expense of undermining the exclusivity of Byzantine imperial authority. There was now another emperor, or tsar to be specific, who was dangerously close in power to the Byzantine emperor.

Zoë gathered people hostile to this surrendering of imperial authority to the Bulgarians, rising to become her son's regent. Mystikos kept his position as patriarch, but Zoë was now at the head of state. One of her first moves was to reject all terms negotiated by Mystikos, as well as the coronation of Simeon. The year 914 was thus a repetition of 913, but this time, instead of marching on Constantinople, the Bulgarians marched on Adrianople, managing to take it over by bribing the heads of the city. Zoë, alarmed, begrudgingly accepted the annual tribute previously negotiated by Leo VI.

Simeon returned once again, uncertain as to whether the Byzantines would live up to Mystikos's concessions. Simeon was well aware that Zoë was hostile toward Mystikos and his concessions to Simeon regarding imperial authority and that she wouldn't let her son, Constantine VII, marry a Bulgarian princess. In fact, Zoë quickly started to forge a plan to completely destroy the Bulgarian Empire by drawing the Serbians, Magyars, and Pechenegs into the conflict.

By 917, the Serbs and Pechenegs had seemingly been drawn into an alliance with Byzantium, and the Byzantines marched into Bulgaria. The soldiers were paid, and commanders were chosen carefully and based on merit. Moreover, Byzantium got some much-needed truce deals with the Armenians and Arabs, who were now free to face the Bulgarian threat.

Things didn't start well for Zoë. The Pechenegs and Serbs failed to honor their part in the war, and the Byzantines had to face the Bulgarians alone. When the day of the decisive Battle of Achelous came, it was just the Byzantines against the Bulgarians. The Byzantines, led by Leo Phokas, pushed the Bulgarians into a retreat.

After stopping to rest his soldiers, who had been battling for a long time on a very hot summer's day, Leo Phokas dismounted his horse. For some reason, his horse quickly ran away. Some soldiers recognized the horse as belonging to their supreme commander and immediately started spreading the word that their great commander had been killed in battle. The battle that had seemed to be going in the Byzantines' favor became a catastrophic defeat, with numerous soldiers trampled and killed in a chaotic withdrawal from the battlefield. Leo Phokas himself perished.

The Byzantine army reassembled in Katasyrtai, a suburb of Constantinople. Simeon was determined not to give the enemy enough time to rest and recuperate, and he organized a night attack on the enemy camp in Katasyrtai, inflicting yet another devastating defeat on the Byzantines. That same year (917), Simeon dispatched a regiment to depose the leader of Serbian Rashka, Petar Gojniković, making Rashka into a sort of client state led by Pavle Branovic, a Serb leader friendly to the Bulgarians.[i]

The campaign of 917 ended inconclusively. Zoë didn't even want to hear about the tribute or the previously arranged marriage between Constantine VII and one of Simeon's daughters. So, the conflict spilled into 918, and this time, Simeon decided not to focus on Constantinople, instead turning to provinces like Thessaly. Macedonia, and Thrace. He just barely managed to recover from years of plundering, which was the main reason why Simeon decided to attack provinces (or themes) that lay far away from Constantinople. In 918, the Bulgarians destroyed Thebes

---

[i] Rashka was an early medieval Serbian state in the southern Balkans.

and reached Corinth, only to return soon to Bulgaria with bountiful loot and numerous prisoners.

## The Macedonian Dynasty under Pressure

By this time, matters in Constantinople had become very murky and confused. In 919, Zoë was removed from the regency, probably owing to the terrible casualties suffered in the war against the Bulgarians. Romanos Lekapenos, the head of the Byzantine navy, which was instrumental in keeping Constantinople safe from sieges, was put in her place with the help of the previous regent, Patriarch Mystikos. Lekapenos married his own daughter to Constantine VII, drastically reducing Simeon's own chances of mingling with the Byzantine imperial family. This prompted Simeon to launch yet another campaign. He was determined to conquer the city of Constantinople, hoping to obtain much-needed naval help from the Arabs. The Arabs, however, didn't make it, as they were stopped by the more powerful Byzantine navy. So, Simeon camped for a while near the Dardanelles and returned to Bulgaria.

Romanos Lekapenos on a coin.[38]

Lekapenos managed to fend off the Bulgarian and Arab threats, convincing the young Constantine VII (who was sixteen years old at the time) to promote him to the rank of co-ruler in 921. Romanos Lekapenos, as we can see, wasn't really content with being the regent of the young emperor; he wanted to become the main man himself. He also convinced Constantine VII to accept Christopher, Lekapenos's own son, as a legitimate heir.

Lekapenos was a shrewd political player, as he was able to draw Serbian Rashka into conflict with Bulgaria. During his annual campaigns in the Byzantine Empire, Simeon regularly left his western borders with Serbian Rashka unguarded. Having been installing client rulers there for quite some time, Simeon was certain that his rear was safe while he was campaigning in Greece.

However, the current ruler of Rashka, Zaharija Pribisavljević, spent a lot of time in Constantinople (he might have been a protégé of the current emperor, Lekapenos) and was previously captured and held in captivity by Simeon when Zaharija tried to take power from another Serbian ruler, Pavle Branovic. Simeon believed that Zaharija had, for all intents and purposes, turned into a good Bulgarian client ruler, and when Branovic started to show signs of weakness and a growing alliance with the Byzantine Empire, Simeon removed Branovic and brought Zaharija to the head of Rashka. Simeon believed that during Zaharija's years of captivity in Bulgaria, he had gained a Bulgarian-friendly attitude. Zaharija wasn't put in a dungeon. He had been under a sort of house arrest, and his rank and dignity had been completely respected by Simeon.

However, Zaharija remained friendly to the Byzantines, and this proved instrumental in 923. While Simeon was in the Byzantine Empire, plundering as usual, Zaharija gathered Serbian forces to strike into Bulgaria. Simeon learned about the plot and sent two of his ablest generals to quench the rebellion. Both, however, were killed in the rugged mountains of Rashka, their heads and armor sent to Lekapenos.

Determined to crush the Serbs, Simeon settled the matters in Greece and turned to Rashka, which was quickly ravaged and turned into a wasteland. Then, Simeon turned to Croatia, which was more unified than Rashka, with significant naval forces. The Bulgarians managed to penetrate deep into Croatia, but due to the challenging and unknown terrain, they fell into a trap and were decimated by the Croatian king, Tomislav, in 926.

Simeon never abandoned his grandiose plans and high hopes, planning yet another excursion into the Byzantine Empire and a potential alliance with the Arabs. However, it was not to be, as he died, probably due to a heart attack, in 927.[i]

---

[i] Hupchick, Dennis P. Simeon's Campaigns for Imperial Recognition, 894-927. The Bulgarian-Byzantine Wars for Early Medieval Balkan Hegemony: Silver-Lined Skulls and Blinded Armies,

# The Inevitable Decline of Bulgaria

The great expansionist period of Bulgarian history essentially ended with Simeon's death. The Bulgarian Empire, although fairly powerful immediately following the death of Simeon, would gradually succumb to the same problems faced by the Byzantine Empire: internal strife and external threats. These issues gradually weakened the Bulgarian Empire.

When military and political command is surrendered to strong personalities, the road is open for the perversion of dictatorial, autocratic power. What then ensues is periods of relative stability, thanks to the prominence of leaders who merit adoration, but also periods of chaos when less honorable people take power. This happened in ancient Rome. The republic laid foundations that were finally shattered by powerful people like Julius Caesar, Octavian Augustus, and Tiberius. And the same thing happened to Bulgaria. The Bulgarians had their share of fame, wealth, and strength, and after Simeon died, the historical pendulum shifted and marked a drastically different period of Bulgarian and Byzantine history.

# Constantine VII and the Succession Crisis

Although already mature, even by modern standards, Constantine VII was only formally the emperor of the Byzantine Empire. Romanos Lekapenos and his family firmly held the imperial reins. Lekapenos knew how to keep the Bulgarian threat at bay.

Although Constantine VII wasn't ultimately married to a Bulgarian princess, Simeon managed to marry his son Peter to Irene Lekapene, granddaughter of Romanos Lekapenos, in 927. This event mitigated the Bulgarian threat and put an end to conflicts that had been raging since the late 9th century.

While Lekapenos was dealing with the military and politics, Constantine VII mainly spent his time on scholarly pursuits; you may recall that we mentioned him as the author of an important text that gives us a glimpse into a number of important historical topics, such as the Christianization of the Slavs. However, starting in 944, Constantine VII started to profit from the animosities between Lekapenos and his own sons, who hoped to grab some of the imperial power for themselves.

Constantine removed the intruders and assured that future emperors would come from the Macedonian dynasty, to which Constantine VII belonged.

Constantine VII on an ivory plaque.[39]

Constantine VII quickly appointed Romanos II, his son, as co-emperor. Constantine VII died in 959, but the death of Romanos II came quickly in 963, putting the Byzantine Empire once again at the will of court intrigue and a battle of interests among the nobility.

The wife of Romanos II, Theophano, made sure to safeguard their two sons, Basil II and Constantine VIII. She was on friendly terms with the two most powerful men in the Byzantine Empire after the death of her husband: Nikephoros II Phokas and John Tzimiskes. The two men successively became emperors and were closely related to Theophano, who seemed to have had all the reins in her hands.

Nikephoros II Phokas, who came to power after the premature death of Romanos II, was instrumental in the reconquest of Crete, which had been in the hands of the Arabs for a long time. Nikephoros was also instrumental in the empire's eastern conflicts with the Arabs. He participated in the capture of Tarsus (modern-day southern Turkey), which was a starting point for many Arab naval raids. The Byzantines, spearheaded by Nikephoros II Phokas, marched farther south, reaching Syria and overtaking cities such as Antioch, Laodicea, Larissa, and many others. Antioch was a particularly tough nut to crack. The Byzantines planned to besiege the city and use hunger as a weapon against the Antioch defenders.

Nikephoros II Phokas.[30]

Nikephoros II Phokas was assassinated in 969, possibly at the request of Theophano and her lover John Tzimiskes, another important general. It is also possible that the events surrounding the siege of Antioch were to blame. When besieging Antioch, Nikephoros's aim was to make the city surrender. He left Michael Bourtzes and Petros (previously a eunuch servant in the Phokas family) in Bagras Fortress to oversee the siege of Antioch during the winter. Bourtzes and Petros received explicit orders not to attack Antioch, as Nikephoros wanted the city walls to remain intact.

Bourtzes, however, was able to reach the officers in Antioch who were responsible for the city's towers and defense walls. Through bribery, he managed to get himself and a few hundred men into the city, after which the bulk of the Byzantine forces were let in, led by a somewhat reluctant Petros. After learning of Bourtzes's disobedience, Nikephoros had him removed from his post and disgraced. Bourtzes then decided to join or form a plot to kill Nikephoros II Phokas. He might have found enthusiastic supporters in John Tzimiskes and Theophano.[i]

It's possible that Nikephoros II Phokas, due to his illustrious heritage, experience, and merit, was feared by Theophano and that she recognized him as a threat to her young sons. She turned to John Tzimiskes (Nikephoros II was his maternal uncle), another influential and able general who might have been easier to control.

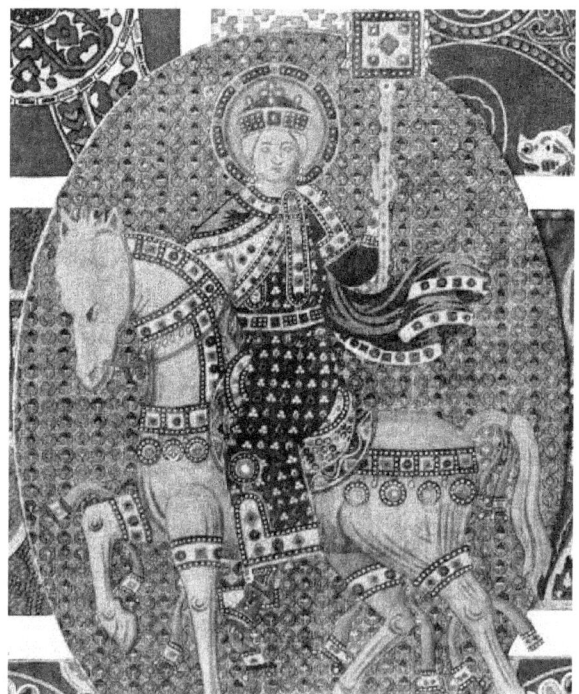

John Tzimiskes, a reproduction of a lost portrait.[81]

---

[i] Krsmanovic, Bojana; Dzelebdzic, Dejan. John Tzimiskes and Nikephoros II Phokas: The background and motives of a premeditated murder. Zbornik radova Vizantoloskog instituta, 2010, 47: 83-120.

It is likely that a plot was devised by John Tzimiskes, Empress Theophano, General Bourtzes, and other conspirators to assassinate Emperor Nikephoros II Phokas. He was murdered in his bedchamber in December 969; his head was severed from his body. Shortly afterward, Tzimiskes was crowned emperor. To deflect blame, he reportedly found scapegoats (their names are not known). The coronation was arranged to take place on Christmas of that same year.

Tzimiskes and Nikephoros II had a troubled relationship. Tzimiskes, a proven and able military strategist in his own right, was removed from his military post as soon as Nikephoros II Phokas became the emperor in 963. Since the earliest days of Rome, the return of a triumphant military general had been one of the most cherished and attended events. A triumph could turn a military general into a figure of veneration, respect, and fear. Tzimiskes wanted to prove himself, this time in the attire of a Byzantine emperor.

## Tzimiskes as Emperor

For all intents and purposes, Tzimiskes continued the same expansionist policy as his predecessor. He managed to fend off the Kievan Rus' (Varangian) attacks in a conflict for supremacy over Bulgaria. Tzimiskes fought the Kievan Rus' leader, Sviatoslav, in a series of battles in Bulgaria. Sviatoslav's forces were finally besieged in the fortress of Dorostolon (modern-day northern Bulgaria), and Sviatoslav was forced to concede. Tzimiskes also captured Boris II, the Bulgarian leader who was forced to side with Kievan Rus' to try and fend off the Byzantines. Bulgaria was officially annexed by the Byzantine Empire.

In the following years, Tzimiskes focused on the situation in the southern parts of his empire, particularly on warfare against the Abbasid Caliphate. He managed to conquer numerous cities, reaching as far as Nazareth and Caesarea (modern-day Israel).

When Tzimiskes died in 976, the Byzantine Empire seemed to have been in a much better position than in the early $10^{th}$ century when Bulgarians, Varangians, and Arabs posed major threats. By the end of the reign of John Tzimiskes, the Byzantine Empire had a firm grip over the Balkans and Mesopotamia.

## Macedonians Back in Power

The sons of Romanos II, Basil II and Constantine VIII, were mature enough to lead the empire by this time. The Macedonian dynasty was ready to return to the scene and lead the Byzantine Empire to the peak of its power. The transition, however, wasn't entirely peaceful or elegant.

By gathering extensive warfare experience and quickly learning the cunning ways of Constantinople's politics and intrigues, Basil II managed to remove opposition after ascending to the throne. It's important to emphasize here that although Basil II and Constantine VIII were formally co-rulers, Constantine VIII, who was younger than Basil II and less interested in politics, was a more peripheral figure, while Basil II took the main stage. He ended the rebellions of two of the most powerful Byzantine families, Phokas and Skleros, in the years following his ascension to power.

Bardas Skleros was the governor of Byzantine Mesopotamia. He learned about John Tzimiskes's death and the subsequent proclamation of Basil II and Constantine VIII as emperors in 976. Skleros immediately gathered an army with the intent of taking the imperial throne by force. He was defeated by Basil II, who had to muster the forces of another eventual contender, Bardas Phokas, who, for the time being, was allied with Basil II. In fact, Phokas dealt the final blow to Skleros in 979. Bardas Skleros went into exile in Iraq, where he was well received by the Muslim authorities.[i]

Basil II feared that Skleros would return at some point to the Byzantine Empire, perhaps aided by the Muslims, who were already a major threat. He considered handing Aleppo to the Muslims if they handed Bardas Skleros over to him. Although this would have been a shrewd move, this offer wasn't received positively by the elite in the Byzantine Empire, especially by Bardas Phokas.

---

[i] Holmes, Catherine. Basil II and the Government of Empire (976-1025). 1999. PhD Thesis. University of Oxford.

Basil II.[88]

After Bardas Skleros was released from Baghdad in 987, he quickly formed an alliance with his previous rival, Bardas Phokas, and another rebellion against Basil II started. Basil II personally commanded his forces in the war against the rebels, and he was helped out by the Russian forces. Basil II was instrumental in the conversion of Russians to Christianity. The first Christian Russian ruler, Vladimir I, was married to Basil's sister, Anna. By 991, Basil II had been able to grind down the rebels completely.

These turbulent events of Basil II's early reign meant that he couldn't stop the Bulgarian expansion. While John Tzimiskes inflicted a devastating blow to the Bulgarians and captured their ruler, the Bulgarian state recovered and managed to reclaim a portion of its previous territory, once again threatening the Byzantine Empire's center of power.

## Basil II, the Uncontested Emperor

Once the internal conflicts were settled, Basil II could turn to the Bulgarian threat. He was determined to end it once and for all. The Bulgarians, led by Emperor Samuel, reclaimed some territories conquered by possibly the greatest Bulgarian ruler, Simeon. During his turbulent early reign, Basil II tried to eliminate the Bulgarian threat, but he was forced to retreat in a humiliating fashion. In 1001, he initiated another offensive, which was much more successful and bloodier.[i] Slowly but surely, Basil II weakened the Bulgarian center of power, cutting the Bulgarians' supply sources and undermining their recovery.

Forced to face Basil II in an open battle, the Bulgarians offered a last resistance effort in 1014 at Kleidion, where they were decisively defeated by Basil II. The Byzantines managed to capture around fifteen thousand Bulgarian soldiers. Almost all were blinded, and a small number of soldiers had one eye spared so that they could guide the mutilated army home.

Over the next few years, Basil II annexed the whole Bulgarian territory to the Byzantine Empire.

## The Reign of Basil II

After defeating the rebels, Basil II sought to further weaken the aristocracy by reducing their influence in regions where they held significant amounts of land. Namely, Basil II forbade aristocrats to hold land and public offices in the same region, thereby mitigating their influence in the areas where they had the most interests.[ii]

Basil II was able to placate, or at least stabilize, support among the poorer segments of society by restoring village lands that had been acquired—often unjustly—by wealthy elites. These estates were returned to their original holders without compensation, and new laws discouraged the further accumulation of land by the aristocracy.[iii]

---

[i] Goodyear, Michael. "Compromised Defense-The Conquests of Basil II." *The Michigan Journal of History*, 5.

[ii] Holmes, Catherine. Political elites in the reign of Basil II. In: Byzantium in the Year 1000. Brill, 2003. p. 35-69.

[iii] Holmes, Catherine. Basil II (AD 976-1025). De Imperatoribus Romanis, 2003.

Basil II was able to assert his dynasty as the sole ruler of the Byzantine Empire, but members of the Skleros family continued to hold high offices. While this wasn't the case for the Phokas family, they still retained some land and status.

Basil II also fought another kind of war. Although he succeeded in removing his great-uncle and closest advisor, Basil Lekapenos, in 985, the latter was able to form an intricate web of alliances and quid pro quo networks within the government, which continued to function and undermine his influence. By 996, Basil II had not only removed the rebels who dared face him in an open battle but also inflicted a final blow to the more tacit resistance that was going on. It was possibly due to this long struggle for power that Basil II was determined to present himself in a truly imperial, imposing, and grandiose style.

Basil II is remembered for his purported war exploit: the blinding of an entire Bulgarian army. While his strategy in Bulgaria was devastating and inhumane, Basil II also knew the importance of solid civil governance and conquest by culture. He was able to fortify the frontiers of his country, not only through conquest and military command but also through religious, cultural, and political influence.

At the end of his reign, Basil II faced another rebellion, this time fomented by Nikephoros Xiphias, Basil's most important general, and Nikephoros Phocas, in 1021. Xiphias was a major factor in numerous military victories of Basil's reign, including the crushing victory against the Bulgarians at Kleidion in 1014.

The ironlike Basil II was able to crush this last rebellion. Having significantly expanded and stabilized the Byzantine Empire, Basil II died in 1025. Constantine VIII, Basil's younger brother, himself already an old man, came to power after Basil's death.

# Chapter 11: Signs of Destabilization

## Prelude to a Decline

After the death of Emperor Basil II in 1025, the question of succession was simple. Basil II had no offspring and had not prepared anyone to be his successor. So, his younger brother Constantine was proclaimed the new emperor. The accession of Emperor Constantine VIII (r. 1025-1028) to the throne led to the strengthening of the influence of court eunuchs, who were appointed to high positions in the state, which resulted in the return of court intrigue. Whenever the administrative matters were left to the court personnel, whether it be in the times of ancient Rome, the Byzantine Empire, or the Russian Empire, there was a high risk of intrigue, corruption, and mishandling of governmental affairs. This is exactly what happened during the reign of Constantine VIII. Constantine VIII, a son of Romanos II and a child during the reigns of powerful men like Nikephoros II Phokas and John Tzimiskes, lurked in the shadows of his much more powerful brother Basil II for some time. He patiently waited his turn. However, by this point, Constantine VIII had become fairly indifferent to the allure of the imperial throne. Nominally, Constantine VIII reigned for sixty-six years alongside Nikephoros, then Tzimiskes, then Basil, and then for three years on his own. He ultimately left a faint mark on Byzantine history.

Emperor Constantine VIII's reign was short-lived, and before his death, the question of succession arose again, even more seriously this time because he had no sons, only three daughters—Eudokia, Zoë, and Theodora.[i] Since Eudokia had taken monastic vows, Zoë (978-1050) inherited the legitimacy of the Macedonian dynasty, and her husband, Romanos Argyros, Prefect of Constantinople, who was related to Emperor Romanos I Lekapenos (who served as a co-emperor to the young Constantine VII in early $10^{th}$ century), was chosen as the new emperor, in 1028. This decision did not provide a lasting solution to the imperial throne but merely postponed it, as the fifty-year-old Zoë was too advanced in years to bear children.

Romanos Argyros, now Emperor Romanos III Argyros (r. 1028-1034), continued the court policy of the previous emperor, generously granting and bribing the support of the ruling segments of society. In 1034, Emperor Romanos III died under suspicious circumstances, after which Zoë's lover, Michael, was chosen as the new emperor and became her husband.

Michael IV (r. 1034-1041) belonged to the Paphlagonian family, which included several influential figures at court, most notably his brother, John the Orphanotrophos, a powerful eunuch who served as chief minister. Although the family was not of noble origin, they rose to prominence due to the decline in traditional aristocratic influence and the increasing dominance of court intrigue, petty officials, and eunuchs in Byzantine politics. Michael was able to rise quietly through the ranks, eventually beginning an affair with Empress Zoë, which led to his elevation to the throne. Full of ambition to establish their lineage as the new imperial dynasty, they persuaded Empress Zoë to adopt Michael IV's nephew, also named Michael, as her son, ensuring the continuation of the Paphlagonian dynasty.

Wishing to further secure support for their regime, the Paphlagonians promoted their own supporters to high positions in the spiritual centers of the empire and in the military.[ii] One of the family's leaders, the influential eunuch John the Orphanotrophos, attempted to secure the position of patriarch of Constantinople in 1037, but his efforts were blocked by the reigning patriarch and church opposition, preventing the family from

---

[i] Ostrogorsky, *History of the Byzantine State*.
[ii] Kaldellis, *Streams of Gold, Rivers of Blood*.

extending its control into the highest ecclesiastical office. The following year, the Paphlagonians launched an unsuccessful military campaign in Sicily, compromising their position with the army.

After the death of Emperor Michael IV in 1041, his nephew and the empress's adopted son, Michael V, succeeded him. Believing he had enough support in Constantinople, Emperor Michael V banished Empress Zoë under charges of a coup and exiled her to Principo in April 1042. This was followed by the forced exile of the popular Patriarch Alexios. Upon hearing this news, the people of the capital rebelled. A mob led by General Constantine Cabasilas forcibly took Zoë's sister, Theodora, to Hagia Sophia, where they crowned her empress, stripping Emperor Michael V of any remaining legitimacy. The short-lived Paphlagonian dynasty, which had started with court intrigues, ended with public unrest.

Sixty-five days later, Zoë married again, this time to Constantine IX Monomachos, who assumed the imperial responsibilities. He had been previously exiled from the empire by Michael IV but was brought back by Empress Zoë. His rule was shaken by various political, military, and church intrigues, which he tried to overcome.[i] Constantine continued the purge instituted by Zoë and Theodora, removing the relatives of Michael V from the court.

The instability of the throne and the empire made him prone to violent outbursts over suspicions of conspiracy. This caution wasn't unfounded. In 1042, Constantine relieved General George Maniakes from his command in Italy, and Maniakes rebelled, declaring himself emperor in September. He transferred his troops to the Balkans and was about to defeat Constantine's army in battle when he was wounded and died on the battlefield, ending the crisis in 1043.

---

[i] Ibid

**Constantine IX.**[88]

Constantine also waged wars against groups that included the Kievan Rus', the Pechenegs, and the rising Seljuk Turks. Despite the varying success of these campaigns, the Byzantine Empire largely retained the borders established after the conquests of Basil II, even expanding eastward when Constantine annexed the wealthy Armenian Kingdom of Ani.

In 1054, a year before Constantine's death, the Great Schism between the Eastern Orthodox and Roman Catholic Churches took place, culminating in Pope Leo IX excommunicating Patriarch Michael Cerularius. Constantine was aware of the political and religious consequences of such an event and made unsuccessful efforts to prevent it from happening.

# The End of the Macedonian Dynasty

With the death of the ruling couple, Empress Zoë in 1050 and Emperor Constantine IX in 1055, Empress Theodora, as the last legitimate representative of the Macedonian dynasty, assumed power. Despite Constantine IX having already designated a successor, Nikephoros Proteuon, the governor of Bulgaria, Empress Theodora, together with her supporters, seized the imperial palace in a coup, which led to the exile of Nikephoros. The empress then appointed her own representatives to the main positions of the state, headed by the chief minister, eunuch Leo Paraspondylos, while simultaneously dismissing Isaac Komnenos, a powerful and popular military commander, from his position as stratopedarches (a high-ranking military officer).[i]

At the end of August 1056, Empress Theodora died at the age of seventy-six, marking the end of the Macedonian dynasty. On her deathbed and with the influence of her advisor, Leo Paraspondylos, the bureaucrat Michael Bringas was selected as her successor and crowned Emperor Michael VI. Although he had administrative experience, Michael VI lacked military credibility, which soon led to tensions with the army and set the stage for his brief and troubled reign. Leo Paraspondylos continued to exert considerable influence during Michael VI's rule.

Upon ascending the throne, Emperor Michael VI generously distributed promotions to officials in the capital while ignoring promotion requests from the officer corps led by Isaac Komnenos. The military commanders once again tried to secure promotions, this time through eunuch Leo Paraspondylos, but they were again rejected, prompting them to retreat to Asia Minor. On June 8$^{th}$, 1057, in Paphlagonia, they proclaimed Isaac Komnenos as emperor.

---

[i] Ostrogorsky, *History of the Byzantine State*.

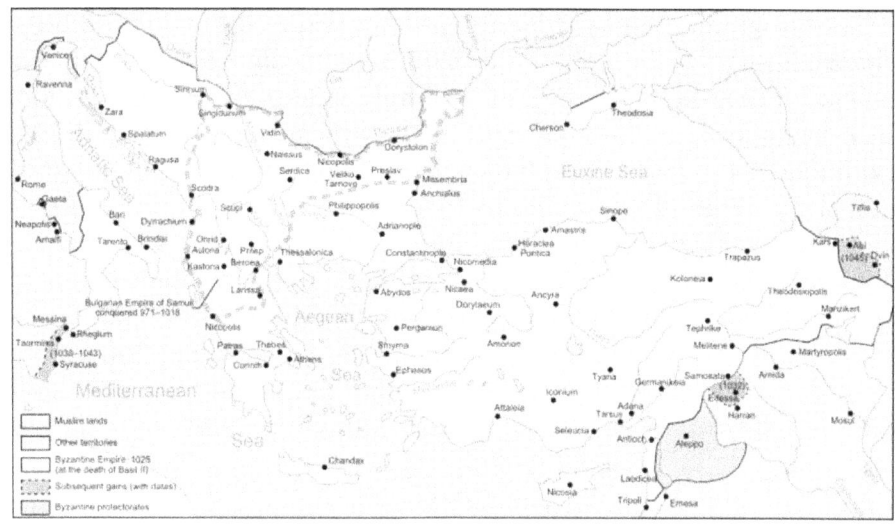

The Byzantine Empire in the 11th century.[84]

# Insurgency

Thanks to the falsification of imperial orders and the provision of their own resources, the insurgents were able to gather a large army. They captured Nicaea and then won a victory over the legitimate forces at Hades. Faced with the possibility of being overthrown, Emperor Michael VI entered into negotiations with the insurgents, offering Isaac Komnenos the title of Caesar and recognition as his successor in exchange for ending the rebellion. However, at the urging of his fellow commanders, Isaac rejected the offer. Although Michael VI had been lawfully appointed by Empress Theodora, his rule lacked broad support, particularly from the military. In contrast, Isaac, a respected general with strong backing from the army, was a compelling alternative to the unpopular emperor.

Meanwhile, during the negotiations between the emperor and the insurgents, the people of the capital were won over to the side of the insurgents, thanks to Patriarch Michael Cerularius, which led to Michael VI's abdication and departure for a monastery where he spent the rest of his life. Constantinople was then peacefully occupied by the insurgents on August 31st, which was followed by Isaac Komnenos's coronation as emperor on September 1st, 1057.[i]

---

[i] Ibid.

Once in power, Emperor Isaac I promoted the accomplices who had helped him gain power, after which he implemented reforms aimed at reducing state expenditures, such as bureaucratic salaries and pensions, which had been increasing since the reign of Emperor Constantine VIII, who frequently awarded court titles and was lenient toward church estates, often at the expense of the military.[i] Due to reforms that encroached on the wealth of individuals and the church, Emperor Isaac I quickly lost popularity among the ruling strata of society, which, combined with his poor health, led to his abdication in November 1059. His accomplice in the rebellion and the president of the Senate, Constantine Doukas, was crowned the new emperor. Upon taking power, he annulled all of Isaac I's decisions regarding the abolition of dignities and fiscal measures.

The year after Constantine died, the capable and brave General Romanos IV Diogenes took power. The new emperor fought against the Seljuks until his defeat and capture at the Battle of Manzikert in 1071. Romanos IV managed to negotiate with the Seljuks and returned to Constantinople. However, during his absence, Constantine's son, Michael VII Doukas, became the sole ruler. A civil war ensued, in which Michael was officially confirmed as the ruler while Romanos retreated, believing in assurances of his safety. However, Romanos's eyes were gouged out, and he died from the injuries he sustained in 1072.[ii]

Michael VII Doukas's reign was characterized by numerous rebellions. Two claimants to the throne from military aristocracy circles emerged, one from Europe and the other from Asia Minor. Nikephoros Bryennios entered his native Adrianople as a counter-emperor in 1077 and marched on Constantinople. His namesake, Nikephoros Botaneiates, also advanced on Constantinople with the support of the Seljuks. Botaneiates entered Constantinople first, seized the throne in 1078, and married Empress Maria, the wife of his predecessor.

The Byzantine Empire was in chaos, and a struggle among generals for supreme power began. The most capable proved to be Alexios Komnenos, a nephew of Emperor Isaac I. He was not only an excellent military commander but also a talented politician, which distinguished him from his uncle Isaac and the unfortunate Romanos Diogenes. With him, a more than century-long period of rule by the Komnenos dynasty (1081–

---

[i] Ibid.
[ii] Ibid.

1204), one of the most glorious in Byzantine history, would begin.[i]

## Internal Problems

The period of dynastic change signified the worsening of problems that were typical of Byzantium due to its geographical and political circumstances. Since the emperor was the head of the state and directed the executive power, he always faced two problems. The first was the need for capable people to fill important positions, especially those in the military. However, the most capable individuals were also ambitious, and as such, they represented a potential threat to legitimate power in the event of an open rebellion. The second problem was the need for authority through official institutions, but there was the caveat that emperors had to find ways to maintain personal control over them; otherwise, the rulers would be sidelined themselves.

To manage potential threats to their rule, Byzantine emperors often marginalized or sidelined relatives—especially siblings—who might challenge dynastic stability. While earlier Roman emperors often involved their families in succession, systematic dynastic rule became more formalized under Alexios I Komnenos, whose reign marked the rise of family-based governance as a political norm. Additionally, emperors sought to limit the power of ambitious generals by frequently transferring them to commands far from their native regions, thus preventing them from building regional power bases.

A similar dynamic existed in the Roman Republic, where the Senate attempted to manage military power through a system of checks and balances. Over time, however, powerful generals such as Gaius Marius, Pompey the Great, and Julius Caesar eroded these controls. Julius Caesar famously crossed the Rubicon from Cisalpine Gaul, initiating a civil war that ultimately led to the end of the Roman Republic and paved the way for the imperial system under Augustus.

The plotting of conspiracies was most pronounced among members of prominent families who had extensive networks and connections with members of other significant families and military officers. They had the necessary unity to seize supreme power, and on those occasions, they presented a representative around whom they rallied all available resources. The household guard, or family retainers, initially formed the

---

[i] Kaldellis, *Streams of Gold, Rivers of Blood*.

nucleus of the forces, after which the common people joined the rebellion. To expand the rebellion, the pretenders sought to broaden their circle of supporters, which invariably included military leaders living in Constantinople and the provinces, demobilized soldiers, and prisoners in the capital.[i]

Following a well-conceived plan of conspiracy, the right moment for defection from imperial authority would be seized, as any attempt at usurpation was doomed to fail as long as the reigning emperor resided in the capital, except in the case of Emperor Michael V. Usurpations in the capital typically occurred when the emperor left Constantinople accompanied by the imperial guard, leaving the court unprotected in the event of a coup.[ii] In the provinces, the rebels had more opportunities to act, especially when the main army, led by the emperor, suffered a defeat against the enemy it was fighting (such as Bardas Phokas in 976 and Caesar John Doukas in 1071) or when the army was deep in enemy territory on campaign (such as Leo Tornikios in 1047). The most reliable method was securing the main command over the army (such as Alexios Komnenos in 1081).

It is also important to keep in mind that internal fluctuations either encouraged or indirectly enabled external crises. The loss of territory necessitated the mobilization of the army to the hotspot, leaving the rest of the empire's territories vulnerable, especially at the other end of the empire. Similarly, internal disputes provided additional reasons for foreign powers to dismember or plunder the empire's borders. Also, considering that the emperor had to worry about usurpers, it was extremely difficult to organize his departure from Constantinople to adequately address a military crisis. To make matters worse, even if a commander managed to successfully handle a military incursion, his success would position him as a pretender to the throne, reducing the chances of his re-engagement.

## External Problems

The turbulent period in Byzantium following the death of Emperor Basil II marked a turning point, particularly in terms of foreign policy. At the time, the Eastern Roman Empire extended across Asia and Europe, with outposts in southern Italy, placing it at the intersection of three rising spheres of influence: the Latin West, the Islamic world, and the Slavic and

---

[i] Ibid.
[ii] Ibid.

steppe regions. These neighboring powers began to grow in strength during this period, reshaping the geopolitical balance in and around the empire.

In the Balkans, the Hungarians occupied border towns such as Belgrade, and the Slavic population, primarily the Bulgarians and Serbians, rose up in rebellion against Constantinople. Similarly, border tribes like the Pechenegs and Cumans raided border territories and plundered towns. Although the situation in the Balkans was serious, it was the least critical compared to other border areas. By far, the most severe situation was in the East with the fall of Anatolia, which was never fully brought back under Byzantine control. In the West, the Normans strengthened their position, causing Byzantium to lose all its possessions in Italy.

At the beginning of the 11th century, southern Italy was divided between the Byzantine Empire and coastal duchies on the Tyrrhenian Sea, which were partially dependent on Byzantium to some extent due to help with defense against the Lombards from the interior. Beginning in the 9th century, Sicily had belonged to the Arabs. In 1018, Basil II sent Basil Boioannes as the catepan (regional leader of the Byzantines in Italy) to consolidate imperial authority in Italy. Boioannes's administration from 1018 to 1028 marked the peak of Byzantine power and influence in Italy.[i] The emperor planned to proceed from there to liberate Sicily from Arab rule, but his death in 1025 thwarted his plan. The catepan George Maniakes would have more success (though briefly) in that endeavor.

Maniakes was sent by Emperor Michael V in 1038 to conquer weakened Sicily due to internal conflicts among the Kalbid emirs. Maniakes had success at the start, liberating the eastern part of the island with Messina and Syracuse. However, Constantine IX Monomachos, who took the throne in 1042, relieved him of his duties. Maniakes died fighting Constantine IX's forces in 1043 after declaring himself emperor and marching on the capital.[ii] With Maniakes's departure, the Zirids, a dynasty from northern Africa, returned to Sicily, and all the wars that were fought further weakened this area, making it easier prey for the future Norman conquerors, who finally expelled Byzantium from Italy in 1071 by capturing Bari.

---

[i] Ostrogorsky, *History of the Byzantine State*.
[ii] Kaldellis, *Streams of Gold, Rivers of Blood*.

The arrival of the Normans began in the 1040s when they came as a mercenary army fighting for all warring sides in Italy. From 1042 to 1059, they became independent conquerors, establishing themselves in Apulia and Capua. However, the turning point came in 1059 when the pope recognized two Norman leaders, Richard of Aversa and Robert Guiscard, as the rulers of the conquered territories, marking the final confirmation of the Norman presence.

The Great Schism of 1054 between the Eastern Church and Western Church led to a change in the attitude of the new pope, Nicholas II, toward the Normans. The pope wanted to use them to expel the Byzantines from southern Italy. Because of this, the pope went to Melfi, where a synod was held, and Robert was proclaimed duke of Apulia, Calabria, and Sicily. In return, he swore loyalty to the pope and promised an annual tribute. After that, Robert conquered all of Calabria and Apulia and expelled the Byzantines from Italy.

However, the Normans were primarily ambitious opportunists and adventurers, so they seriously considered Byzantium's offer to join the empire just a few decades later. An offer was given by Michael VII Doukas, who had just risen to the throne after Romanos had suffered the loss at the Manzikert. The emperor sought help from Robert in the fight against the Turks. To this end, he sent letters with proposals, offering a marriage between his newborn son and Robert's daughter. Robert Guiscard aligned himself with the Byzantine Empire through a marriage agreement. His daughter was betrothed to Constantine Doukas, the son of Emperor Michael VII, and sent to Constantinople to be raised in the imperial court. However, this arrangement collapsed in 1078 when Nikephoros III Botaneiates seized the throne in a coup. As a result, Michael VII was forced to become a monk, and Robert's daughter was confined to a convent, ending the proposed alliance.[i]

The instability in Byzantium led the Byzantine emperors to use extreme measures to form alliances. The imbalance in the empire caused these alliances to fail. Provoked by this outcome, the Normans entered a phase of expansion, conquering Calabria and Apulia by 1071 and Sicily from 1061 to 1091. However, their influence in Byzantine politics would continue. The Normans, hungry for territory, embarked on plundering and conquest campaigns in Byzantine territory, first in the Balkans and

---

[i] Houben, *Roger II of Sicily*.

then within the Levant. Numerous conflicts culminated in a direct clash with Byzantium (1081–1085).

This westward expansion did not limit itself only to the Normans; it also manifested in the Crusades, during which western European states created kingdoms in the Middle East. The weakening of Byzantium allowed the West to pursue opportunistic policies, and it also showed that Byzantium lacked the capacity to liberate its former territories (many of them holy places for Christians) from the influence of Muslim states. On the other hand, the Great Schism prevented the coordination of the Roman Church with the rest of the Christian world, hindering unity in religion and identity between the East and West.[i]

A similar situation occurred in the East. The eastern part of the empire, centered in Antioch, was one of the most significant cities of the empire. Antioch was important as a strategic border point for the eastern part of the Byzantine state, and it housed the center of the Byzantine army, which was in close proximity to Arab Aleppo, the Arab center of Syria. The governor of this city and region held the title of dux, and in the transitional period between the Macedonian dynasty and the Komnenos dynasty, this title served as one of the stepping stones to usurp the throne. For this reason, due to instability, it was practically a title for pretenders to the throne.

The dux and domestikos (a regional leader) of the East, Philaretos Brachamios, a member of the old Armenian family Brachamios, rebelled against Michael VII Doukas and held Antioch, Edessa, Germanikeia (Marash), and Melitene himself. This area, after the Battle of Manzikert and before the Turkish conquest, was only nominally part of Byzantium.[ii] The Seljuks took advantage of the division within the state and finally conquered the city in 1085.

After Tughril Beg's victory over the Buyids in Baghdad in 1055, the Seljuks emerged as restorers of Muslim unity under the Sunni caliphate. In Byzantium, the Seljuks were hired as mercenaries by various rival Byzantine generals in their behind-the-scenes struggles for the imperial throne in Constantinople, so the Seljuks gradually gained increasing influence over Byzantine political affairs. At the same time, they controlled an ever-growing number of territories in Anatolia as allies of the

---

[i] Fouracre, *The New Cambridge Medieval History Set*.
[ii] Ostrogorsky, *History of the Byzantine State*.

Byzantine emperor.[i] The Eastern province followed the same route.

The court intrigue and uncertain successor to the throne caused ruling families and capable military leaders to shift their focus to Constantinople. In effect, this weakened the state, making it a far easier target for emerging regional powers. Their emergence was nothing new, but in the past, Byzantium had the strength not only to endure these attacks but also to spread its territory. This fall from grace would continue in the future, with capable leaders managing to salvage some things. In the end, though, the Eastern Roman Empire paid the final price of having conspiracies and court intrigue.

---

[i] Ibid.

# Chapter 12: The Great Schism

The Great Schism, which occurred on July 16th, 1054, between the Roman Church and the Patriarchate of Constantinople, was a canonical separation and the end of a single liturgical community. This event was the result of numerous factors and cannot be viewed from a single perspective or considered as having a single cause. The fact that the two sides, which were once united through one church, would completely distance themselves and thereby divide the church was evident long before 1054. In the 11th century, problems and tensions between the East and West reached their peak, but they had been developing throughout the Early Middle Ages and increased over time.

The schism of 1054 is one of several schisms that occurred in the history of the Christian Church, but this one was final. The causes are numerous and complex, and they should be studied in historical, political, theological, and cultural contexts. The Eastern and Western parts of the Roman Empire primarily differed in language, tradition, and theological crises, and all of these differences arose due to the different circumstances in which they developed. Because of the division of the Roman Empire, iconoclasm, and various theological and dogmatic issues, the final schism of the Christian Church into the Orthodox Church and the present-day Catholic Church occurred.

The division between the Eastern and Western Churches.[85]

Both churches wanted their independence, perhaps not initially. Over time, they became aware of their political situations, which pushed them in different directions. Over time, the Eastern and Western Churches developed in such different ways that they were unable to share common social conditions or exert meaningful influence over each other's political realities.[i] While Byzantium was surviving incursions from the Muslim states, Rome was becoming a player in the medieval European states that were forming around it.

Factors that would have allowed for the unity of the Christian world had been lacking for centuries. As previously mentioned, the Western and Eastern Churches developed in parallel but were shaped by differing ideological frameworks. In Byzantium, the concept of caesaropapism—where the emperor held significant authority over ecclesiastical matters—was a major factor necessitating coordination between the disputing sides. The Eastern Roman emperor often acted as the de facto authority in

---

[i] Jedin, Dolan, and Holland, *History of the Church.*

appointing patriarchs, a practice that became increasingly problematic as Byzantium lost control over its territories in and around Italy. With the loss of these possessions, Byzantium could no longer guarantee peace and security to Rome, which had to seek another protector and thus become a political player that would build its own sphere of influence. As the West solidified behind the Frankish Kingdom, it forced Byzantium to bring the Slavs under its influence. After bringing the Southern Slavs to heel, the next step was, of course, to Christianize Russia within the patriarchal authority of Constantinople.

## Precursors to the Schism

After difficult battles against the Muslims, the Byzantine Empire preserved its central territories and simultaneously blocked the path to Christian Europe while securing its status as a great power. However, the price was high. The extent of the empire significantly diminished in these battles, but Byzantium strengthened within its new borders. The influx of new external forces into the empire, as well as many reforms, revitalized the aging late Roman state. Following the Heraclian restoration, Byzantium was forced into many defensive wars against migrating peoples who settled on its borders, such as the Avars and Bulgars. After these victories, they began their offensives in Asia and the Balkans to regain some of the lost territories.

The Roman Empire, which had been united in the past, could not be revived. Although under the influence of Roman traditions and ideas, Byzantium transformed into a medieval Greek empire, while the West witnessed the formation of Germanic kingdoms in the former territories of the old empire. The future development of Byzantium was guided by the Greek culture and language, creating a new identity for the Byzantine Empire.[i]

In 751, Byzantine rule in northern and central Italy was destroyed. Ravenna was conquered by the Lombards, and the Exarchate of Ravenna ceased to exist.[ii] The newly established Frankish Kingdom, which grew into a new power, assumed the role of protector of the pope. In January 754, Pope Stephen II personally traveled to the Frankish Kingdom across the Alps to forge an alliance with the Frankish king. This act symbolically turned the pope away from the Byzantine emperor. In response, the

---

[i] Cleenewerck, *His Broken Body*.
[ii] Ostrogorsky, *History of the Byzantine State*.

Byzantine emperor separated the Hellenized southern Italian provinces of Calabria and Sicily and the province of Illyricum, which belonged to the Roman Church, from Rome.

Another factor in the distancing of the East from the West was iconoclasm. This deepened the rift between the two ecclesiastical centers and eventually pushed Rome out of the Greek East and Byzantium out of the Latin West. This meant that both the universalism of Byzantine imperial power and that of the Roman Church began to lose ground.

This rift was further deepened by the coronation of Charlemagne as emperor and the establishment of the Papal States.[i] A process was initiated to resist the influence of the East on the West and vice versa. The first step in resisting was taken by the iconoclast Constantine V, who subordinated southern Italy and a large part of the Balkan Peninsula to the Patriarchate of Constantinople. All these were immediate causes and indirect triggers, but direct confrontation between the Patriarchate of Constantinople and Rome could only begin after overcoming the iconoclastic crisis.

## The Photian Schism

In 857, Photius became the patriarch of Constantinople. He ascended to this position after Emperor Michael III removed the previous patriarch, Ignatius. Photius was one of the most skilled diplomats and politicians to occupy the seat of the patriarch. The two candidates for the seat sought approval from Pope Nicholas I, an ambitious and energetic politician. A significant obstacle for Photius was that he was a layman who had been consecrated (ordained) within five days without adhering to church tradition. The pope sent his envoys to investigate the matter. To secure his position, Photius bribed the papal envoys, but the pope discovered this and dismissed them. Subsequently, in 863, the pope ordered Photius to abdicate from the seat of patriarch.[ii]

Constantinople was attempting to establish an autonomous position. In light of these events, Photius decided to excommunicate the pope and accused the Roman Church of heresy. The patriarch went further and criticized the Western Church for errors in matters of liturgy and church discipline. He attacked the Western doctrine of the Holy Spirit

---

[i] Orlandis, *A Short History of the Catholic Church*.
[ii] Cleenewerck, *His Broken Body*.

proceeding from the Father and the Son (*ex Patre Filioque*). Thus, Photius, whom the pope thought he could summon as a defendant, accused Rome of heresy in the name of orthodoxy.

In 867, a synod held in Constantinople under the emperor's presidency excommunicated Pope Nicholas I, rejected the Roman doctrine of the Holy Spirit's procession as heresy, and declared Rome's interference in Eastern Church affairs unlawful. A letter from the patriarch that extensively addressed and harshly condemned the different teachings and customs of the Roman Church, especially *Filioque*, was sent to the Eastern patriarchs.

Photius was supported by Emperor Michael until the emperor was killed in 867. The new emperor, Basil I deposed Photius and exiled him to a monastery. Ignatius was reinstated as the patriarch of Constantinople. Pope Nicholas I, having proven his ability to influence the affairs of the Eastern Church, distanced the Byzantines from Rome. This event is considered one of the factors leading to the Great Schism and is known as the Photian Schism.[i]

## Political Reasons for the Schism

When discussing the political causes of the Great Schism, one must return to the factor that perhaps led to the greatest tensions in the disagreements between the East and the West: the elevation of the Patriarchate of Constantinople. This elevation occurred in 451 as a result of the Council of Chalcedon and its famous Canon 28, which placed all the territory of the Byzantine Empire under the jurisdiction of Constantinople. Such a provision was unacceptable to Pope Leo I, who refused to accept it since Constantinople was attempting to present itself as the "New Rome." For these reasons, Constantinople was transformed into the main patriarchate of the Christian East, becoming a rival to the Roman papacy. During a period when the Roman Church was distancing itself from the Byzantine Empire, the Eastern Church increasingly identified with Byzantium, leading Rome to turn toward the Frankish and German emperors. This cooling of relations caused a weakening of the church and its unity.

Another significant problem with church universalism between the East and West was the issue of church primacy.[ii] The primacy of the Roman

---

[i] Jedin, Dolan, and Holland, *History of the Church*.
[ii] Cleenewerck, *His Broken Body*.

Church played a crucial role in uniting the universal church, which had previously been divided. The Western Church believed that Jesus Christ chose his apostle Peter as his successor and the builder of the church's foundation as an institution on Earth. By this logic, the task entrusted to Peter was not temporary or limited by his lifetime; rather, it represented the establishment of a church heritage. Peter became the first bishop of Rome, and his successors inherited not only his title but also the right of primacy, establishing themselves as the pinnacle of the church, justified by the will of Christ. In this way, the Roman Church assumed the role of the center of unity for the universal secular church based on heritage.

Rome invoked its historical rights and ecclesiastical primacy based on legacy, which increasingly irritated Byzantium as the years passed. Byzantium wanted to be independent and structure the church according to its own terms rather than being dependent on every decision made by the Roman Church. The moment that highlighted the obvious problem of primacy was the attempted alliance between Rome and Byzantium against the Normans, as it revealed the struggle for primacy between the two sides.

Furthermore, in addition to the question of primacy, the Gregorian reform aimed at freeing the church from secular power and achieving autonomy. This movement was named and endorsed by Pope Gregory VII.[i] He attempted to resist the previous practices of kings, princes, and other nobles who distributed bishoprics and abbeys and exploited the church for financial gain (simony). One of the goals of the movement was to secure the right of church elections to ensure the independence of areas under religious authority. Additionally, the Cluniac reform awakened a sense of dignity and independence in the church and spiritual life. These reforms helped the Christian Church achieve a sense of value and awareness in the West.

One of the major supporters of the Cluniac reforms was Pope Leo IX, who, with the help of Cardinal Humbert, held a series of church synods across Europe from 1049 to 1053.[ii] At these synods, issues such as lay investiture, simony, and clerical marriages were condemned. These decisions soon clashed with the religious views of Constantinople and its patriarch, Michael Cerularius. Pope Leo IX politically attempted to claim southern Italy, which was gradually being taken from Byzantium by the

---

[i] Orlandis, *A Short History of the Catholic Church*.
[ii] Jedin, Dolan, and Holland, *History of the Church*.

Normans, provoking a conflict between the East and the West.

One of the political causes of the schism included iconoclasm.[i] Iconoclasm was initiated by the emperors of the Syrian (Isaurian) dynasty: Leo III the Isaurian, Constantine V, and Leo IV.[ii] They promoted an aristocratic view of the Christian faith, emphasizing the search for the absolute and direct worship of God without the mediation of images and other religious symbols. The movement was partly started because the veneration of icons, supported by the successful sale of saintly images by some monasteries and their art workshops, had reached a level of superstition. Icons were purchased for vows and prayers and celebrated as family saints (sometimes even taken as wedding godparents instead of living people). There were also frequent cases of consuming paint scraped from icons as medicine for various illnesses. Although iconoclasm might be theological and cultural in nature, the iconoclastic conflicts were political since they are remembered as a kind of religious war between the two sides of the church.

In 726, Emperor Leo III decreed a ban on icons in the Byzantine Empire, leading to catastrophic conflicts, the destruction of mosaics and frescoes, the devastation of monasteries, and the persecution and murder of iconophile priests. The conflicts intensified, necessitating military interventions. In 730, an imperial edict by Leo III, influenced by Jewish and Islamic models and church circles that were negatively disposed toward icons, banned the cult of religious images or icons.[iii]

The Seventh Ecumenical Council was convened in 787 under the auspices of Patriarch Tarasius and consisted of eight sessions held from September 27th to November 23rd of the same year. Empress Irene and her son participated in the final session of the council.[iv] The council was attended by over three hundred bishops, including two papal legates, who also signed the council's resolutions. Tarasius rejected the conclusions made in 754 against icons and refuted the iconoclast arguments against the veneration of images inspired by scripture and church tradition. He also defined icons as religious doctrine, viewing them as pictorial representations of Christ, the Mother of God, angels, and saints. He believed they should be allowed because such expressions of faith led to

---

[i] Besançon, *The Forbidden Image*.
[ii] Ostrogorsky, *History of the Byzantine State*.
[iii] Ibid.
[iv] Ibid.

the emulation of the religious ideals depicted in them. It was concluded that worship or *latreia* belonged only to God and was different from the veneration of images or proskynesis, which relates to the prototype and is not equated with God. Those who opposed the conclusions were treated leniently if they showed repentance for their earlier iconoclastic ideals.

During the 9th century, iconoclasm resurged, but after the decisions of the aforementioned council, it eventually succumbed to pressure. The West did not succumb to the temptations of iconoclasm; there, images were initially valued for their moral value. Thus, iconoclasm became one of the disagreements between the West and the East.

The lack of sustained communication and linguistic misunderstandings led to the separation of these two sides. Greek was the official language of the Christian Church for the first three centuries, but at the turn of the 3rd century, Latin was introduced into literature and liturgy. By the end of the 4th century, under the influence of Carthage, Western liturgy fully adopted Latin. This language barrier not only created a rift between the East and the West but also led to mutual suspicion and distrust at a time when the church was shaken by heresies and theological disputes.[i] The division deepened with the introduction of differences in discipline and rites.

## Theological Causes

From the formation of the Christian Church up until the Great Schism of 1054, numerous differences emerged between the eastern and western parts of the empire. The theological, doctrinal, and cultural differences that separate the Western and Eastern Churches are not simple issues. Differences exist even among Eastern churches, with some Eastern theologians highlighting distinctions between Russian doctrine and their own. It is generally accepted that the two churches, Eastern and Western, diverge in the doctrines of the procession of the Holy Spirit from the Father and the Son, the primacy and infallibility of the Roman bishop, purgatory, and the two most recent Marian dogmas, especially the Immaculate Conception.

Debates on the doctrine of the procession of the Holy Spirit arose as early as 381 at the Second Ecumenical Council in Constantinople, where the teaching of the third divine person was condemned as heresy. Further disagreements over the Holy Spirit led to the insertion of the Filioque

---

[i] Cleenewerck, *His Broken Body*.

clause into the Nicene-Constantinopolitan Creed.

The Nicene Creed of 381 in its original form states: "I believe in the Holy Spirit, the Lord and Giver of Life, who proceeds from the Father, who with the Father and the Son is worshiped and glorified." In the West, this part reads: "I believe in the Holy Spirit, the Lord and Giver of Life, who proceeds from the Father and the Son, who with the Father and the Son is worshiped and glorified."[i]

The addition "and the Son" (Latin *Filioque*) was added in the West by the 5th century at the latest. This doctrine was based on the theological works of some Eastern Church fathers, such as Saint Cyril of Alexandria, who believed that everything the Father has, he has given to his only begotten Son, thus making the Son consubstantial with the Father. However, many Eastern theologians and churchmen did not find these explanations sufficient. This doctrine clashed with their beliefs, making the Filioque a significant point of contention between the two sides. Patriarch Michael Cerularius was also among those who considered the addition of the Filioque to the Nicene-Constantinopolitan Creed a violation and heresy by the Roman Church, claiming that this act caused it to lose its jurisdiction in the Church of Christ.

Regarding the sacraments, the greatest difference was celibacy. The West reformed the church to enforce celibacy, prohibiting priestly marriages, while the East disagreed, allowing such marriages. Further differences are found in the sacrament of chrismation (confirmation) and baptism. In the East, it was typically performed by an ordinary priest, whereas in the West, this duty was usually carried out by a bishop. Contrary to Catholic belief, Eastern Orthodox theologians hold that chrismation must be repeated for an apostate returning to their faith. Orthodox theologians also criticized the West for deviating from Orthodox teachings on several other points.

A problem also arose in the sacrament of the Eucharist. The West used unleavened bread for the sacrament, which Eastern churchmen criticized, along with the fact that Holy Communion was not given to small children. Another important point of controversy regarding the sacraments was the prayer to the Holy Spirit, which is believed to transform the bread and wine into the body and blood of the Savior. This act, known as the epiclesis, is absent in the Western Church, which

---

[i] Cleenewerck.

believes that the transformation occurs during the recitation of Christ's words and does not require the mention of the epiclesis. Eastern priests, however, believe that the words of the epiclesis must be spoken and that this alone is necessary for the transformation.[i]

Another difference between the two theologies and churches regarding the sacrament is related to confession, specifically the penance imposed by the priest on the penitent during confession. In the Eastern Church, penance or epitimia served instructive purposes, while in Catholic doctrine, it served exclusively for forgiveness.

Finally, Eastern and Western churchmen disagreed on the issue of church councils. Some Eastern Orthodox theologians viewed the Trullan Council as ecumenical, calling it the Fifth-Sixth Council, as it completed the decisions of the Fifth and Sixth Ecumenical Councils.

In conclusion, the theological issues that were prevalent just before the Great Schism of 1054 were old issues that had divided churchmen since the time of Photius and earlier.

The theologian differences were not, as sometimes portrayed, the cause of the Great Schism. They were given as the official reasons, but the actual cause was the separation of political and cultural development. The political separation was finalized with the loss of Byzantine territory in Italy and with Rome's decision to seek protection from the Frankish Kingdom. The cultural separation happened parallel with politics, with exposure to different influences and differences in language.

The Great Schism was one of many crises between two churches, which permitted their relationship before and after 1054. Their distancing continued well into the $13^{th}$ and $14^{th}$ centuries. The Great Schism ended without a solution and served as a final, symbolic step in the separation between the East and the West that still exists.

---

[i] Cleenewerck.

# Part Four:
# Decline and Fall
# (1081–1453 CE)

# Chapter 13: The Komnenian Dynasty and the Crusades

## Introduction

During the reign of Empress Theodora, who was the last representative of the Macedonian dynasty, there were discussions about the future successor. Given that Theodora was elderly and her death was expected any day, and since she had no offspring, the logical step was to choose a new emperor. Many tried to influence Theodora regarding the appointment of her successor. Finally, Leo Paraspondylos convinced Theodora to name Michael Stratiotikos as the new emperor. Theodora's decision was accepted without any opposition by the patriarch of Constantinople.

Michael was shortly dethroned, and his successor, Isaac Komnenos, reigned from 1057 to 1059.[1] After just two years of rule, Isaac abdicated, and Constantine X Doukas was chosen as the new emperor. The exact reason for his abdication is unknown, but it is presumed that he was a victim of a conspiracy by those dissatisfied with his rule. His short rule would probably have stayed as a footnote in history books if he had not been the first ruler of the Komnenian dynasty, one of the most influential royal families in Byzantine history.

---

[1] Ostrogorsky, *History of the Byzantine State*.

Constantine X Doukas died in 1067, leaving his underage son, Michael VII Doukas, as his heir. His mother, Eudokia Makrembolitissa, assumed the regency. With the empire facing serious military threats, Patriarch John VIII Xiphilinos granted her permission to remarry, overriding a clause in Constantine's will. Soon afterward, she married the general Romanos Diogenes, who was crowned Emperor Romanos IV.

During his reign, Byzantium faced numerous problems. The problems faced by the empire were partially caused by the growing influence and power of the aristocracy, which weakened the empire's military structure. A series of weak rulers after the strong soldier-emperor Basil II disbanded the large armies and stockpiled gold in Constantinople in order to hire mercenaries. Despite the severity of losing Italy, the Byzantine Empire suffered its greatest catastrophe in Asia Minor. The Seljuk Turks, who were primarily focused on fighting the Fatimids of Egypt, launched a series of raids in Armenia and eastern Anatolia, which was the main source of Byzantine recruits. By reclaiming much of this region, the Komnenian emperors halted the Turkish advance in Anatolia for over two centuries. In the process, they laid the groundwork for the Byzantine successor states of Nicaea, Epirus, and Trebizond.

## Diminishing Influence in Italy

The Byzantine Empire's last stronghold in Italy fell under Norman control in 1071. The Seljuk Turks attacked Byzantine cities, forcing Romanos to engage around 200,000 soldiers to expel the Turks from Asia Minor. A conflict arose between the Byzantines and Turks near Manzikert in Armenia.[i] During the battle, the Normans deserted, leaving the Byzantines on their own. Initially, they had the advantage, and victory was within reach. However, a false rumor spread by Romanos's rival, Andronikos Doukas, that said the emperor had been killed in the battle led to the army scattering in fear. Many historians believe this defeat was pivotal, as it allowed the Turks to expand farther into Asia Minor and deal a heavy blow to Byzantium from which it never fully recovered.[ii] At the Battle of Manzikert in 1071, the Turks captured Emperor Romanos IV Diogenes and overtook Anatolia, which severely weakened Byzantine influence in the east. There were some exceptions where Byzantine control was still

---

[i] Haldon, *Byzantium at War*.
[ii] Ostrogorsky, *History of the Byzantine State*.

strong, most notably in Lesser Armenia.[i]

Romanos IV's successor, Michael VII Doukas, appealed to Pope Gregory VII for assistance against the advancing Seljuk Turks. However, Gregory was deeply engaged in the Investiture Controversy with Holy Roman Emperor Henry IV and did not respond to the request. This appeal, though unsuccessful, foreshadowed future attempts by Byzantine emperors to seek Western support, particularly during the era of the Crusades.

The Komnenian dynasty played a pivotal role during this period. From the accession of Alexios I Komnenos in 1081 to the death of Andronikos I in 1185, the Byzantine Empire experienced a period of political, military, and economic revival, often referred to by historians as the Komnenian restoration.

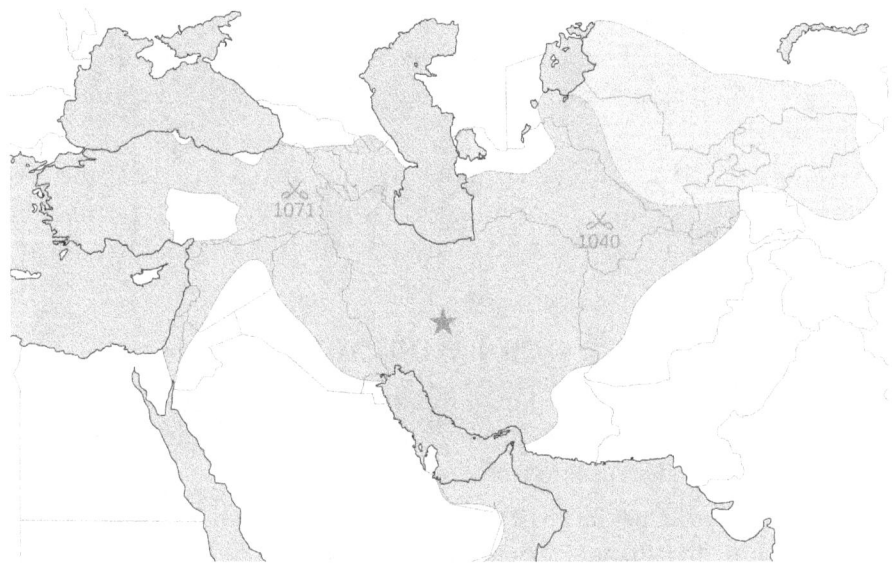

Expansion of the Seljuks in the 11ᵗʰ century.[86]

## Michael Doukas

Michael VII Doukas, son of Constantine X, became emperor during a period of profound crisis. Byzantium faced external threats and internal instability, particularly after the disastrous Battle of Manzikert in 1071, which led to the loss of Asia Minor to the Seljuk Turks.

---

[i] The western part of the former Armenian Kingdom, known as Armenia Minor.

Michael was seen as a weak ruler, ceding much of the empire's administration to the powerful eunuch Nikephoritzes. The latter imposed harsh taxation policies while mismanaging military funding and court spending. These failures caused widespread public discontent, particularly among the military, which led to desertions and mutinies. The devaluation of Byzantine currency under Michael's reign earned him the mocking nickname "Parapinakes," meaning "a quarter less," symbolizing the economic decline.

Meanwhile, the empire's control over the Balkans weakened. The Bulgarians remained restive, and Slavic groups such as the Serbs began asserting greater autonomy, signaling future challenges to imperial authority.

Facing mounting pressure, Michael VII abdicated in 1078 and entered monastic life. While he was spared, Nikephoritzes became a scapegoat for the regime's failures. He attempted to flee to Heraclea Pontica, but he was captured and handed over to the new emperor, Nikephoros III Botaneiates.

Nikephoros III's rule lasted only a few years. In 1081, he was overthrown by Alexios I Komnenos, who started the Komnenian dynasty—a powerful line that would restore some of Byzantium's former strength over the next century.[i]

## Alexios I Komnenos

Alexios I (r. 1081-1118) was one of the most powerful nobles of his time. He focused on stabilizing the empire and restoring Byzantine authority in Anatolia through alliances and military campaigns.

Alexios I Komnenos already had a distinguished military career by the time he rose to the throne, having served under Emperors Romanos IV Diogenes, Michael VII Doukas, and Nikephoros III Botaneiates. He and his politically astute mother, Anna Dalassene, conspired to depose Nikephoros III. Anna, who came from the influential Dalassenos family, was a formidable figure in her own right and maintained close ties with Maria of Alania, the former empress to both Michael VII and Nikephoros III.

---

[i] Angold, *The Byzantine Empire, 1025-1204.*

To strengthen the plot, Anna persuaded Maria to adopt Alexios as her son, a move that enhanced his legitimacy and tied him to the Doukas dynasty. Maria's chief concern was securing the succession for her own son, Constantine Doukas, whose position was increasingly threatened under Nikephoros III. As part of the scheme, Anna might have staged a diversion by seeking sanctuary in the Hagia Sophia, as she allegedly feared a plot to blind her sons. While she occupied the emperor's attention, Alexios and his brother Isaac rallied support and marched on Constantinople, successfully ousting Nikephoros III.

Following Alexios's coronation in 1081, Constantine Doukas was named co-emperor, and Anna Dalassene was granted the prestigious title of Augusta. The Komnenoi and the Doukai forged a temporary alliance, which was further solidified by Alexios's marriage to Irene Doukaina. Although Irene was young and less politically seasoned than Maria of Alania, she became an important figure in the new dynasty. Maria remained at court and likely retained some influence early in Alexios's reign.

With the birth of John II Komnenos in 1087, Alexios secured a direct heir, marking a turning point in his personal authority. Over time, both Anna Dalassene and Maria of Alania receded from political life, and Alexios began to rule more independently. His reign was marked by persistent military challenges, but unlike several of his predecessors, Alexios successfully reasserted control over both the court and the provinces, founding the Komnenian dynasty and ushering in a period of relative stability and military revival for the Byzantine Empire.

The Byzantine Empire was threatened by the Normans under Robert Guiscard, who invaded the Balkans from the west. After inflicting a defeat on Emperor Alexios I Komnenos, Robert was forced to return to Italy to support Pope Gregory VII, who was facing a crisis in Rome. In his absence, Robert left his son, Bohemond, to lead the Norman campaign. Given their mutual opposition to Robert and Pope Gregory, Emperor Alexios found a strategic ally in Henry IV of the Holy Roman Empire, who was then locked in conflict with the papacy during the Investiture Controversy.[i]

---

[i] Ostrogorsky, George, *History of the Byzantine State,* Rutgers University Press, 1969, p. 337.

The Byzantine emperor also made an alliance with the Venetians. What Byzantine troops lacked on the ground was even worse at sea, so the aid from the Venetian fleet was of great importance. With their help, Alexios managed to defeat the Norman armies led by young Bohemond, marking the beginning of the Komnenian restoration.

Shortly after, the Pechenegs, a nomadic group, invaded the empire from the north. Alexios allied with the Cumans, another nomadic group, and with their help, they annihilated the Pecheneg horde in 1091. By making clever alliances and using his advantages at the right moment, Alexios proved himself to be a great leader with good political connections.

Alexios Komnenos.[87]

During Alexios I's reign, the Byzantine Empire established standing armies known as *tagmata* to respond rapidly to threats. These units consisted of both cavalry and infantry. The Komnenian era focused on recruiting professional, disciplined, and well-equipped soldiers. Reforms also enhanced logistical support for the army, ensuring a steady supply of provisions, arms, and equipment, which enabled Byzantine forces to operate more effectively and for longer periods of time. Additionally, fortifications, roads, and communication networks were developed to facilitate rapid movement. Armies also saw improvements in siege warfare techniques, including the use of more advanced siege engines and tactics. Military manuals and strategic treatises were also revised during the Komnenian period, providing guidelines for future commanders.

In 1095, Alexios sent an appeal for military aid to Pope Urban II. Unlike their predecessors, Michael Doukas and Pope Gregory, they struck an alliance. Pope Urban II answered the emperor's call the same year and convened the Council of Clermont in France, calling for participants to fight in a holy war to recapture Jerusalem from Muslim control. He preached that Christians should unite in a fight against Muslims, the common enemies of the Christian faith, and promised to provide indulgences to those who enlisted.

The earliest wave of Crusaders, led by Peter the Hermit, a priest from France, was composed largely of peasants, the poor, and indebted individuals seeking spiritual rewards and escape from hardship. Undisciplined and poorly equipped, they suffered heavy losses shortly after entering Asia Minor. The main force of the First Crusade followed later and was made up of prominent feudal nobles, such as Duke Godfrey of Bouillon, Count Raymond of Toulouse, Count Hugh I of Vermandois (brother of French King Philip I), Duke Robert of Normandy, and Bohemond of Taranto. These leaders agreed to support Emperor Alexios I Komnenos in reclaiming Byzantine territories in Anatolia in exchange for safe passage and logistical support. The Byzantine general Tatikios was assigned to accompany the Crusaders, helping coordinate their efforts in the early stages of the campaign.[i]

Alexios demanded every Crusade leader to take an oath of homage when they arrived in Constantinople, and his former enemy Bohemond was no exception. French knight Hugh de Payen, with eight more

---

[i] Ostrogorsky, George, *History of the Byzantine State,* Rutgers University Press, 1969, p. 342.

followers, swore an oath to be a sort of police escort for the Crusaders. They got a house near the Temple of Solomon, defining them as Knights Templar.

Despite facing financial challenges and resorting to drastic measures, such as melting down church artifacts and selling church lands, Alexios achieved important military victories. He recovered Nicaea, Rhodes, and Ephesus. Alexios's popularity was affected by his financial measures, but he managed to be consistently successful in mitigating dissent by the time of his death in 1118.

In terms of foreign policy, the period between the death of Basil II and the rise of Alexios I Komnenos marked the collapse of Byzantine authority in Asia Minor, the loss of imperial possessions in Italy, and a noticeable weakening of control in the Balkans. These setbacks coincided with the disintegration of the socioeconomic and military systems that had sustained the empire under Basil II. Alexios I's efforts to restore imperial stability were based on new foundations, with his administrative, military, religious, and cultural reforms forming the pillars of the revitalized Byzantine state.

After Byzantium freed itself from danger, it was time to confront new threats. This time, Alexios successfully dealt with Prince Vukan of Serbia (Rashka), who was disrupting the internal security of Byzantium with his raids. Alexios had to be content with the apparent submission of Prince Vukan in 1094, as old Byzantine allies, the Cumans, invaded the empire, causing disorder all the way to Adrianople. This time, they were led by Constantine Diogenes, who claimed the imperial crown. Alexios scattered them and captured the pretender. He finally managed to establish peace in the European part of the empire and intended to focus on Asia Minor. However, during this period, a Crusader army approached Byzantium on its way to Jerusalem, looting Hungary and the Balkan lands along the way.[i]

---

[i] Haldon, *Byzantium at War*.

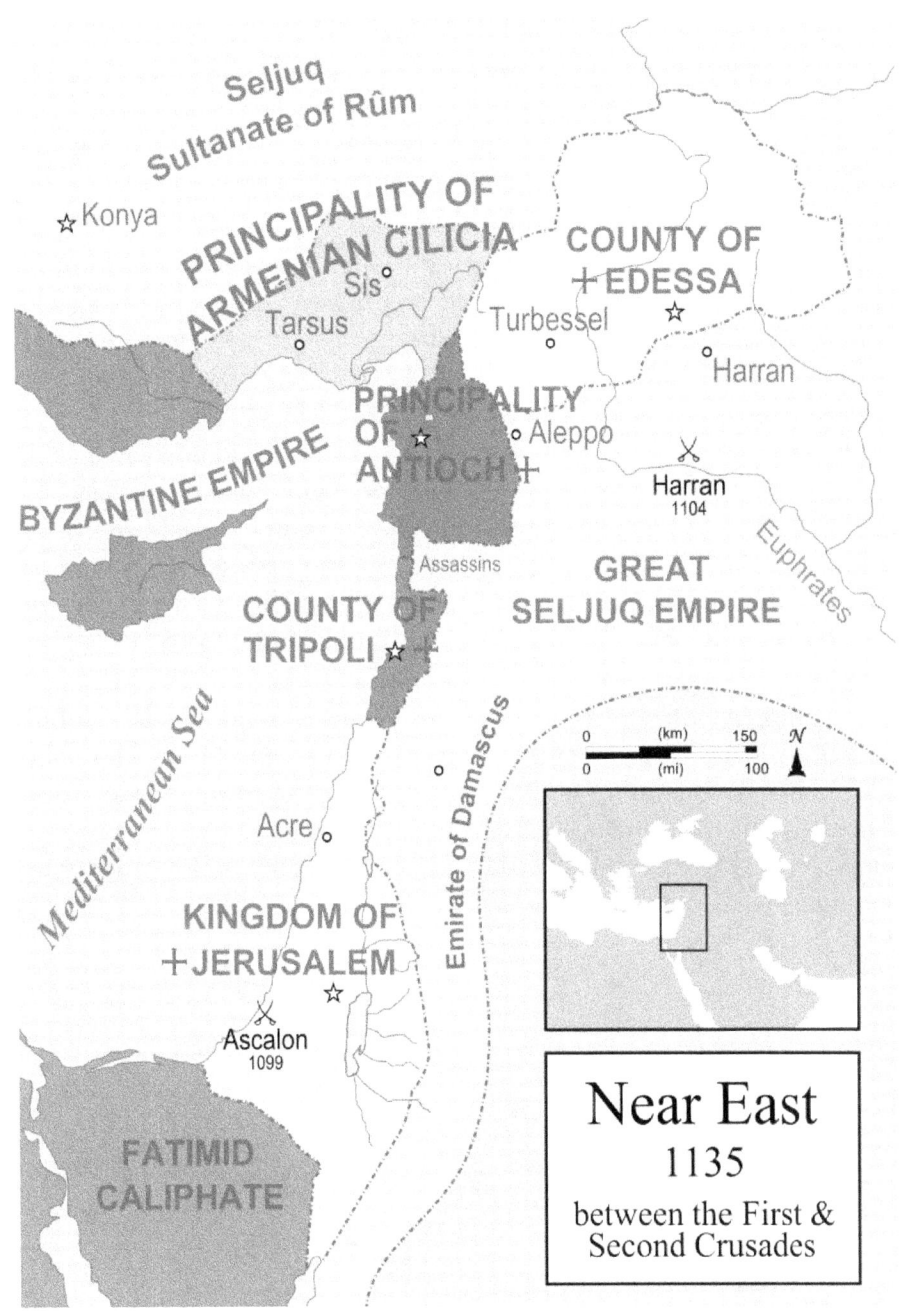

The Crusader States in the Holy Land.[88]

# John II Komnenos

John II Komnenos succeeded his father, Alexios I, in 1118 and is often regarded as one of the most successful rulers of the Komnenian dynasty. The third child and first son of Alexios and Irene Doukaina, John was recognized early on as heir, and by 1108, during negotiations with Bohemond of Taranto, he was already acting in an authoritative role.[i]

Known by the epithet Kaloïoannēs, often translated as "John the Good" or "John the Beautiful," John was praised more for his spiritual and moral character than for his physical appearance. William of Tyre, a contemporary, described him as physically unattractive, further reinforcing the view that the nickname referred to his virtuous nature.

John's reputation for justice, discipline, and piety echoed that of his father, Alexios I, and his mother, Irene Doukaina, whose marriage was noted for its stability and mutual devotion. John himself was deeply spiritual, frugal, and famously moderate in his exercise of power. He notably refrained from excessive cruelty or the theatrical punishments common in medieval courts, earning him comparisons to Roman Emperor Marcus Aurelius.

To secure alliances in the volatile Balkans, Alexios arranged for John to marry Piroska of Hungary (later known as Irene) in 1104. This union strengthened Byzantine ties with Hungary at a time when Slavic groups, particularly the Bulgarians and Serbs, were asserting greater autonomy. John's reign brought relative stability and prosperity to the empire, continuing the Komnenian revival.

---

[i] Mullett and Smythe, *Alexios I Komnenos*.

John II Komnenos, a mosaic from Hagia Sophia.[89]

After taking power, John II did not have time to rest. The Seljuks attacked the southern part of Thrace in 1119. John decided on an offensive, which he launched with his friend John Axouch. He achieved success in the war, crowned by the capture of Sozopolis in 1120. However, John did not have time to celebrate because he had to confront the Pechenegs, who had crossed the Danube and started looting the surrounding areas in 1121. After defeating them and pacifying Rashka, new problems continued with the Serbs, who still frequently rebelled against the Byzantine Empire by allying with Hungary, which was becoming an increasingly strong power in the Balkans and the Adriatic.[i]

The Hungarians eventually decided to attack to establish their influence and power in the Balkans, and in 1128, their army destroyed the fortress of Belgrade. After that, the Byzantine heavy cavalry won a victory over Hungary, following their advance farther south. John's army

---

[i] Ostrogorsky, *History of the Byzantine State*.

successfully continued to advance to Zemun. Hungary was forced to agree to peace. John could finally focus on Asia Minor after stabilizing the Balkans.[i]

John decided to reclaim territories in Anatolia and launched several campaigns toward this goal. The first few were not very successful due to the military situation and conspiracies in Constantinople, which forced the emperor to abandon the campaigns. However, after the death of his wife Irene, John returned to Anatolia. There, he conquered Gangra and Kastamonu in 1135 and achieved victory against the Danishmends, one of the Turkic tribes from Anatolia. After that, he decided to continue his path of conquest and set out for Antioch. On the way, he had to confront the Armenian Principality of Cilicia in 1137. After this victory, the cities of Tarsus, Adana, and Mamistra fell. Finally, John reached Antioch, which he captured after a short siege.[ii]

John did not solve some problems solely with force but also with skillful diplomacy. This is best seen when, after the establishment of Norman rule in Sicily, he established a blockade of the Norman fleet in cooperation with Germany and Pisa.

The emperor planned another campaign and the reconquest of territories in Palestine, but he was prevented by an accident that occurred during a hunting expedition. During the hunt, he was attacked by a wild boar, and in the struggle, he was pierced through the arm by a poisoned arrow. The only option was amputation, which he refused. John died on April 8th, 1143.[iii]

## Manuel I Komnenos

Emperor John II Komnenos decided to bypass his older son Isaac and leave the crown to his youngest son, Manuel.[iv] The new emperor, Manuel I, was born in 1118 and ascended the throne as a young man. It's not entirely clear why John II decided to bypass Isaac and the other older brothers of Manuel, who was fourth in line to inherit the throne. It is possible that Manuel was perceived as the most suitable for the throne out of all his brothers.

---

[i] Haldon, *Byzantium at War*.
[ii] Ostrogorsky, *History of the Byzantine State*.
[iii] Ibid.
[iv] Ibid.

Manuel I Komnenos was described as a ruler with a fierier temperament than his father and a much greater inclination toward Western customs than his predecessors. He introduced new forms of behavior, such as participating in knightly tournaments. Additionally, at the beginning of his reign, more and more foreigners arrived in the empire, causing internal unrest. He adopted his father's political goals, although he pursued them much more recklessly. He also continued to develop good relations with Germany and married King Conrad III of Germany's sister-in-law, Bertha of Sulzbach.

Manuel Komnenos with Maria of Antioch, his second wife.⁴⁰

At the very beginning of Manuel's reign, he faced the same problem as his grandfather Alexios: the arrival of the Crusaders, which included his brother-in-law Conrad.ⁱ It is worth noting that relations between the French king and the Byzantine emperor were quite strained to the point

---

ⁱ Riley-Smith, *The Crusades*.

that there was even speculation about a Crusader takeover of Constantinople. Following his grandfather's example, Manuel negotiated the handover of territories that were previously under Byzantine control and then transferred the Crusader army across the Bosphorus to avoid disturbances.

While the Byzantine Empire was preoccupied with the Crusaders in 1147, Norman King Roger II launched a devastating naval raid, capturing the island of Corfu and sacking the wealthy cities of Corinth and Thebes, which were Byzantine territory. On his way back to Germany, Conrad stopped in Constantinople and promised to help Manuel in the fight against the Normans. Venice also joined the anti-Norman coalition, but Byzantium managed to recapture Corfu in 1149.[i]

Manuel I Komnenos planned a military campaign against Norman territories in Italy, with Emperor Conrad III of Germany initially promising support. However, Roger II of Sicily skillfully used diplomacy and exploited unrest in Germany, forcing Conrad to withdraw. Roger secured alliances with the Kingdom of Hungary and the Serbian principality of Rashka. By 1149, the Grand Župan of Rashka had incited revolts and openly defied Byzantine authority. Roger also sought to ally with King Louis VII of France, who had previously entertained plans for a crusade against Byzantium, though the French knights ultimately refused to take part in such a campaign.

The European states were divided into two camps; on one side were Byzantium, Germany, and Venice, and on the other were the Normans, France, Hungary, and Rashka, with the support of the papacy. After Conrad III resolved the internal problems, everything was ready for the campaign in Italy. However, before the campaign could begin, Conrad died and was succeeded by Frederick I Barbarossa, who was not interested in a joint attack. From that point on, Germany and Byzantium began to diverge in their policies.

After the death of King Roger II of Sicily in 1154, Emperor Manuel I Komnenos launched a campaign to reassert Byzantine influence in southern Italy. His fleet arrived at Ancona in 1155. With the assistance of defecting Norman vassals, Manuel's forces managed to seize control of several key cities in Apulia despite operating with a relatively small army.

---

[i] Angold, *The Byzantine Empire, 1025-1204.*

However, the initial success of the Byzantines did not please their old allies, Frederick Barbarossa and Venice. The following year, Roger's successor, William I, launched a counterattack. The ensuing Battle of Brindisi saw Byzantium inflict a heavy blow to the Normans, forcing them to make peace in 1158. After this successful campaign, Manuel increasingly promoted the idea of restoring the Roman Empire to the time of Justinian, although he lacked the means to undertake such a venture.

Manuel achieved great success in the Latin states. First, he subdued Armenian Prince Thoros, who had entrenched himself in Cilicia, incorporating him among the "Roman servants" in 1158. He then moved against Antioch and its ruler, Reynald. Reynald had to acknowledge the supreme authority of Byzantium and pledge his assistance. After this, the king of Jerusalem, Baldwin III, visited Manuel and placed himself under his protection.[i] This was a significant achievement, as Manuel had secured the loyalty of the Latin states, which viewed Byzantium as their protector.

In his dealings with Hungary, Emperor Manuel I Komnenos continued his father's policy of intervening in succession disputes. Initially, he supported Stephen IV and Ladislaus II—uncles of Hungarian King Stephen III—during a period of civil strife. Although Manuel attempted to install a pro-Byzantine ruler, Stephen III ultimately retained the throne.

To solidify Byzantine influence, Stephen III's younger brother, Béla, was sent to Constantinople, where he was raised in the imperial court and was betrothed to Manuel's daughter. Manuel granted Béla the prestigious title of despotes and named him heir to the Byzantine Empire. In addition, Béla was promised governance over Dalmatia and Croatia, further tying the two realms together politically.

Béla was invited to Constantinople to negotiate terms of an alliance, but the talks ultimately failed since Stephen III resisted Byzantine influence. In response, Manuel I prepared for a military confrontation, dispatching troops to intimidate Hungarian factions. In 1164, he personally led a campaign across the Danube and successfully established Byzantine control over the region of Sirmium, securing key territories between the Sava and the Danube. Concurrently, a Byzantine army was sent to Dalmatia, where it managed to seize several coastal cities, further extending imperial influence in the western Balkans.

---

[i] Angold.

However, due to health problems, Manuel left the campaign, and command was taken over by his nephew, Andronikos Kontostephanos. Andronikos Kontostephanos, through his strategic maneuvers, managed to force the Hungarian army into battle near the fortress of Zemun in the Sirmium region. After the successful battle, the territories of Dalmatia, Croatia, Bosnia, and the Sirmium region fell to Byzantium in 1167.[i]

During this period of conflict with Hungary, the Byzantine Empire was shaken by frequent uprisings in Rashka. Manuel suppressed these rebellions and replaced the local lords, but his actions did not completely resolve the issues. In 1166, Stefan Nemanja became the lord of Rashka. Stefan also turned against the emperor and dealt him a severe defeat. However, after Hungary's defeat, Rashka was left without a powerful ally in its fight against Byzantium. In 1172, Manuel marched on Rashka with a large army. Nemanja abandoned resistance and became a Byzantine vassal.[ii]

New problems emerged when Sultan Kilij Arslan II of the Seljuk Sultanate of Rum consolidated his power in Asia Minor and failed to honor previous agreements with Byzantium, including the return of several cities and potential military cooperation. In response, Emperor Manuel I Komnenos launched a major campaign in 1176, intending to capture the Seljuk capital, Iconium. Kilij Arslan, recognizing the threat, attempted to negotiate, but Manuel refused.

Anticipating Manuel would take the same route he had used in 1146, the sultan prepared an ambush near the ruined fortress of Myriokephalon, where the terrain was narrow and ideal for a trap. The Seljuks also scorched the land, destroying food and water sources along the way. Despite warnings from his commanders, Manuel ordered a frontal assault into the pass, where the Seljuk forces had already positioned themselves.[iii]

Though the Byzantines managed to break through the pass and avoid total annihilation, they suffered heavy losses in manpower and lost much of their siege equipment. As a result, Emperor Manuel I was forced to abandon his campaign against Iconium. The defeat was significant enough that some contemporaries compared it to the catastrophe at Manzikert in 1071. This turning point ended Byzantine hopes of reclaiming central

---

[i] Ostrogorsky, *History of the Byzantine State*.
[ii] Ibid.
[iii] Haldon, *Byzantium at War*.

Anatolia.[i]

Despite all his previous military successes, Manuel's grand plans remained unattainable. His constant warfare exceeded the available strength and resources, creating many enemies. Moreover, during Manuel's reign, the military grew in importance. The population became increasingly impoverished, and more people chose to join the army. To meet the need for recruiting soldiers, Manuel increasingly used the pronoia system, granting land to nobles in exchange for military service, which accelerated the process of feudalization, weakened the state, and undermined the country's defensive strength. These processes would further weaken the Byzantine Empire after Manuel's death.

## Alexios II Komnenos and Andronikos Komnenos

After Manuel's death, his twelve-year-old son Alexios II ascended the throne, with Empress Maria of Antioch acting as regent.[ii] However, this arrangement faced opposition from other members of the dynasty and the populace due to Maria's Latinophile policies. Andronikos Komnenos also opposed these policies, thus emerging as an ideal candidate for the new emperor.

Andronikos reached Constantinople without significant resistance; the only opposition came from Protosebastos Alexios, who attempted to block the Bosphorus.[iii] However, a revolt erupted in Constantinople, leading to Alexios being blinded and imprisoned. In May 1182, a massacre occurred in the city, resulting in the killing and plundering of a significant portion of the Latin population.

Alexios II fell under Andronikos's influence and was forced to sign a death warrant for his mother. Subsequently, Alexios II became a co-ruler, although this was merely a façade. Two months later, Alexios II was strangled by Andronikos's supporters, and Andronikos officially became the Byzantine emperor. He immediately began addressing the issues of bribery and corruption with strict and merciless measures. He also targeted the nobility, using violent means against them, which created even

---

[i] Ostrogorsky, *History of the Byzantine State*.
[ii] Ibid.
[iii] A protosebastos was another title denoting a high court position.

more enemies. Furthermore, external political problems arose due to the absence of the authority that had characterized Manuel's reign.[i]

By 1181, taking advantage of the political instability following Emperor Manuel I's death, Béla III of Hungary regained control over Dalmatia, Croatia, and the region of Syrmia. With imperial authority weakened, uprisings broke out in Rashka, where the Grand Župan Stefan Nemanja quickly reasserted independence from Byzantine rule. This shift culminated in a joint Hungarian-Serbian invasion of Byzantine territory in 1183. The campaign devastated key cities such as Belgrade, Braničevo, Niš, and Sofia. Nemanja not only secured Rashka's autonomy but also expanded his domain by annexing the strategically vital region of Zeta in what is now Montenegro.[ii]

Asia also faced troubles, with frequent uprisings against Andronikos's rule led by magnate families, particularly the local Komnenians. Their representative, Isaac Komnenos, established independent rule in Cyprus, separating it from the Byzantine Empire. Isaac assumed the imperial title and minted his own coins; he faced no punishment for his actions. Andronikos only executed a few of his friends in Constantinople.[iii]

However, the greatest threat to the Byzantine Empire came from the Normans, who launched a military campaign. They first attacked Durrës in 1185 and then moved toward Thessalonica, occupying Corfu, Cephalonia, and Zakynthos along the way. They reached Thessalonica without significant resistance, where they began a siege by land and sea. The city's defenses were weak, and it was soon captured. After Thessalonica, the Norman army advanced toward Serres. Fears of a Norman conquest of Constantinople grew, and there was mounting dissatisfaction with Andronikos's tyrannical rule.

The crisis reached its peak when Emperor Andronikos I Komnenos ordered the arrest of Isaac Angelos. Isaac evaded capture by taking sanctuary in Hagia Sophia, where he rallied public support and was quickly proclaimed emperor by a mob. Andronikos attempted to flee, likely toward Kievan Rus', but was intercepted by Isaac's supporters and returned to Constantinople. There, he was subjected to brutal torture. His hair and beard were torn out, and his right hand was mutilated. Eventually,

---

[i] Ibid.
[ii] Ibid.
[iii] Angold, *The Byzantine Empire, 1025-1204.*

he was dragged through the city and killed in the Hippodrome before a vengeful crowd. With his death in 1185, the Komnenian dynasty came to an end, marking the close of a pivotal chapter in Byzantine history.[i]

---

[i] Ostrogorsky, *History of the Byzantine State*.

# Chapter 14: The Fourth Crusade and Recovery

## The Fourth Crusade

In letters dated August 15$^{th}$, 1198, Pope Innocent III called for the organization of a new crusade to the Holy Land. Motivated by the inconclusive outcome of the Third Crusade, disappointment with the failed German expedition under Henry VI, and the continued Muslim control of Jerusalem, Pope Innocent aimed to reclaim the Holy Land in full. He also used the opportunity to assert papal supremacy by taking a central role in organizing the Crusader army and positioning the papacy as a dominant force in secular political affairs.[i]

The recruitment for the Fourth Crusade did not proceed favorably. Due to poor papal diplomacy and continuous international instability, the burden of military leadership fell on counts rather than kings. It is doubtful that the Crusade would have been feasible without investments from the church leaders. A recurring challenge of earlier Crusades was the need to raise vast sums of money, which often influenced the direction and effectiveness of the campaigns. In early 1202, a group of French envoys arrived in Venice to negotiate support for the Fourth Crusade. Six knightly envoys, all of whom had taken the cross, signed a contract with the Venetian doge, Enrico Dandolo. According to the agreement, Venice

---

[i] Bartlett, *The Making of Europe*.

would provide ships and logistical support to transport the Crusader army to Egypt, which was viewed as the strategic gateway to reclaiming the Holy Land.[i]

This risky venture left the Venetians without a significant portion of their financial income for a year, as they invested in a project that did not promise secure profit. Moreover, no one could guarantee that enough Crusaders would enroll and adhere to the terms set by the group of leaders. Although the French counts were extremely wealthy and politically powerful, they had no authority to bind anyone except themselves and their vassals. Due to the gamble by both sides, the agreement became a deadly trap.

Upon arriving in Venice, the Crusaders were housed on the island of Lido at the eastern edge of the lagoon, where conditions ranged from comfortable to desperate depending on one's status, wealth, and connections with the nobles' entourages. The estimated number of thirty-five thousand warriors was not reached. According to some estimates, only a third of the total number arrived: just a quarter of the knights and half of the infantry. However, the empty spaces in the ranks of the ships' galleys and boats led to confusion about covering the costs, which had to be met under the contract terms. Thus, the Venetians pressured the Crusaders to honor the agreement.

The first option to attempt to resolve the crisis was for each Crusader to pay for his own transport. Even though this was insufficient, everyone contributed what they could. Most began selling their equipment and property to avoid the shame of being unable to pay the agreed price and keep their word. Despite efforts, the Crusaders still owed about thirty-four thousand marks, around 40 percent. Many Crusaders were left with barely enough to survive the upcoming winter on the island of Lido. Venetian Doge Enrico Dandolo understood how important it was for the main command to maintain its reputation and promote the Crusade's goals.

At one point, in September 1202, the blind Dandolo granted the Crusaders a temporary moratorium on their debt repayment. In return, the Crusaders were to embark on the ready fleet and help the Venetians capture the Dalmatian port of Zadar. The Crusaders would receive a share of the spoils to revive their hopes of settling the remaining debt.[ii]

---

[i] Nicolle and Hook, *The Fourth Crusade 1202-04*.
[ii] Nicolle and Hook.

This move was justified as the first step toward Egypt, which was impossible to reach until spring due to the season.

Pope Innocent III had explicitly ordered the Crusaders, under the conditions of the campaign he had drafted and signed, not to attack, conquer, or destroy Christian lands.[i] However, the circumstances were such that the Crusaders could not adhere to these conditions because the debt had not been fully paid. It was necessary to keep the army from disbanding and the endeavor from collapsing. Within a month of setting out, they had conquered Trieste and Muggia, followed by Pula. The fleet arrived at Zadar on St. Martin's Day, November 11th, 1202, and captured the port.[ii]

## Alexios Angelos and the Agreement with the Crusaders

In the summer of 1202, Alexios Angelos, the son of the deposed Byzantine emperor Isaac II, fled Constantinople and eventually made his way to the court of his brother-in-law, Philip of Swabia, in Germany. There, he learned of the Crusader army gathering in Venice and was advised to offer them an alliance. In exchange for their help in reclaiming the Byzantine throne, Alexios promised substantial military and financial aid, including funding the Crusade and pledging to reunite the Eastern and Western Churches. Burdened by debt and attracted by the offer, the Crusader leaders agreed to support him.

Alexios joined the Crusaders in Zadar in May 1203. At that time, the Crusade nearly came to an end. Almost half of the army balked at the final obligation to restore young Alexios to power. However, persistent arguments convinced the Crusaders to head toward Constantinople, where they arrived on June 24th, 1203. Despite the overwhelming opposing army, Emperor Alexios III refused to surrender, as his subjects did not share the Crusaders' enthusiasm for his nephew. The inhabitants observing the scene did not know who he was and did not express any support, especially when they saw his army was composed of Venetians and Crusaders.

---

[i] Villehardouin, *Memoirs or Chronicle of the Fourth Crusade and the Conquest of Constantinople.*
[ii] Nicolle and Hook, *The Fourth Crusade 1202-04.*

This situation was dire for the Crusader leaders. They were deeply committed and lacked the means to retreat. Open war was their only option.[i]

After successfully achieving naval supremacy in a short but intense battle in Galata and arriving at the gates of Constantinople, the Crusader army surrounded Constantinople's large and strong walls. These walls intimidated the Crusaders but motivated and encouraged the Byzantine army not to surrender a city that had never been conquered since its founding. On July $17^{th}$, the Venetians and the Franks launched a joint attack on the front of the Palace of Blachernae, located in the far northwestern corner where it would be easiest to penetrate the city. Due to intense breakthroughs and fires, which got out of control and destroyed vast areas of the central part of the city, Emperor Alexios III withdrew.

Although the city had not yet been conquered, the emperor's retreat showed the final state of the situation. Emperor Alexios III, distressed, unprepared, and outmaneuvered, decided to flee the city. His officials who remained immediately freed his blind predecessor and brother, Emperor Isaac II Angelos, from prison, reinstating him to the throne. They thought this would halt the attack on the city since Emperor Alexios III was no longer on the throne.[ii]

However, this presented a problem for the Crusaders because Isaac was not mentioned in the agreement with his son Alexios. Nevertheless, the Crusaders fulfilled their part of the agreement, and on August $1^{st}$, 1203, young Alexios was crowned co-emperor in Hagia Sophia.[iii] As soon as he was crowned co-emperor, becoming Alexios IV, he had partially fulfilled the agreed terms with the Venetians by paying off the debts incurred by the Crusaders at a cost of fifty thousand marks and compensation for his own ascension, which amounted to the Crusaders' debt. Thus, Venice and its citizens received almost 100,000 marks.

Unlike his father, who had sufficient support, Alexios IV lacked a political base among the Byzantine ruling circles. Recognizing that the presence of the Crusaders provided him with security, he decided to hire them in Constantinople as his protectors until March 1204, when it was believed that the campaign could resume its path to Egypt. In return, after

---

[i] Nicolle and Hook, *The Fourth Crusade 1202-04*.
[ii] Ostrogorsky, *History of the Byzantine State*.
[iii] Ostrogorsky.

the expiration of the agreement with Venice, he would support them financially for a year and guarantee them a campaign to the East. Once the Crusaders accepted the emperor's proposal, Alexios IV, together with Boniface of Montferrat, Hugh of Saint-Pol, and Henry of Flanders, toured the Byzantine province of Thrace to establish his authority and prevent a counterattack by Alexios III.[i]

Relations in the Byzantine Empire between the Westerners and the Byzantines deteriorated due to increasing disappointment and distrust in the new regime on both sides. With the accession of Alexios IV to power, the political situation worsened. Payments to the Crusaders were delayed, and the sources dried up, as the Byzantines could no longer endure Alexios's impositions that covered the Westerners' protection. Churches were also plundered by the authorities, seizing gold ingots for the same purpose. Among other things, Isaac began to engage in astrology, and Alexios led a debauched life with his Western allies, showing no concern for preserving their dignity in public, which also strengthened the sense of an impending crisis.

Alexios IV Angelos.[ii]

---

[i] Nicolle and Hook, *The Fourth Crusade 1202-04*.

The lack of money to pay the Crusaders and the Byzantines being overwhelmed by defeat, heavy taxation, and the prolongation of the existing order indicated the loss of Isaac's and Alexios's power. Open violence became more common. As the emperors quickly lost track of the events around them, an attack was launched by the anti-Western faction, led by Alexios V Doukas, nicknamed Mourtzouphlos ("melancholic" or "sullen"), who, with the support of the army, civil service, and clergy, successfully overthrew the existing government. On the night of January 27th, he arrested and imprisoned Alexios IV, and soon after, the other emperor, Isaac, died in prison.[i]

In February, Mourtzouphlos's forces continued the war against the Westerners, attempting to crush them. However, when success was lacking in the initial strikes, Mourtzouphlos managed to negotiate with the Crusaders to continue the agreements that had been made with his deposed predecessor, Alexios IV.[ii]

Despite the conciliatory situation, the Crusaders' options were limited since their ships required repairs, equipment, and supplies for people who were seriously endangered because Mourtzouphlos had closed the capital's markets. One must also consider the new Byzantine anti-Western government. The new emperor no longer wanted to negotiate with the Crusaders, and he began preparing an attack and strengthening the city's walls. The severe circumstances pressing on the Crusaders forced them to act quickly; otherwise, their campaign was in danger of collapsing. The option that quickly ripened as the best choice was to conquer Byzantium for themselves, which would open the way to the necessary supplies and resources.

Doges Dandolo, Boniface of Montferrat (a nobleman from northern Italy), Baldwin of Flanders, Louis of Blois, and Hugh of Saint-Pol concluded that conquest was the only choice to preserve the campaign, so preparations for seizing the city, power, and empire began. According to the so-called March Agreement from 1201, all spoils would be collected centrally and distributed so that the final compensation for all the various obligations made by the Venetians, valued at 200,000 marks, would be paid first.[iii] Once this debt was settled, the Crusaders and Venetians would equally share the profit according to the agreement. Women and the

---

[i] Ostrogorsky, *History of the Byzantine State*.
[ii] Nicolle and Hook, *The Fourth Crusade 1202-04*.
[iii] Pears, *The Fall of Constantinople, Being the Story of the Fourth Crusade*.

clergy were to be spared during the looting, and rape and church plundering were strictly prohibited under the threat of death. The future emperor of Constantinople and Byzantium would be chosen by a twelve-member commission—six Venetians and six Crusaders—and he would receive a quarter of the capital and two imperial palaces. Any dealings with Venetian enemies were prohibited, an obvious example of Dandolo's profiteering. If the emperor was chosen from among the Crusaders, the new Latin patriarch had to be a Venetian, indicating secular interference in the election of a church authority.

The remainder of the empire was to be divided by a commission made up of twelve Venetians and twelve Crusaders, with lands distributed as fiefs among the Crusader leadership, including the newly elected emperor. This new political agreement was secured by deciding that the army would remain in Byzantium for another year until March 1205, delaying the campaign to Egypt for the fourth time since 1202.[i] Anyone who broke the terms of the agreement would be punished with excommunication.

## The Crusader Attack Begins

The Crusader attack began on April 9th with amphibious warfare techniques, used with the help of Venetian ships, which acted as troop transports and assault siege engines. The attack reached its peak on April 12th when, during desperate hand-to-hand combat, the walls were breached, and a bridgehead was established on a critical part of the battlefield inside the fortifications. The Crusaders cleared a path into the city by killing and looting, making no distinction between soldiers and civilians.[ii] Fearing a counterattack, the Crusaders set a fire that quickly spread from the north to the south of the city.

As the anti-Western faction lost ground, Emperor Mourtzouphlos realized that the opponents had won, and he fled the city during the night. By April 13th, there was no serious resistance to the Crusaders, signaling that the city had been conquered. The victory might not have been achieved without the incredible naval skills of the Venetians and the engineering ingenuity that allowed the ships to be turned into battle towers.

---

[i] Nicolle and Hook, *The Fourth Crusade 1202-04*.
[ii] Nicolle and Hook.

The fall of Constantinople to the Crusaders.

For three days, Crusader leaders allowed their troops to vent their anger, greed, and relief in an orgy of looting. The pillage and killings turned beautiful Constantinople into a heap of ruins. A contemporary source noted that even the Saracens would have shown more mercy than the Crusaders.[i] The original pious goal of the Crusaders had been lost. The fall of Constantinople might never have gained such a notorious reputation for dreadful barbarism if the victors had continued their campaign to the Holy Land the following spring.

The new state system in Byzantium was to be implemented according to the agreement that the Venetians and Crusaders had made in March 1204. It was assumed that Marquis Boniface of Montferrat would be elected emperor. His personal and military capabilities and Byzantine connections made him worthy of this honor, but the doge did not favor this, as he desired a less prominent person. Since the Frankish camp was not united within itself like the Venetians were, he managed to secure the election of Count Baldwin of Flanders as the new emperor.[ii] He was crowned emperor of the Latin Empire on May 16th in Hagia Sophia, and the Venetian Thomas Morosini became the first Latin patriarch of Constantinople.

---

[i] Nicolle and Hook.
[ii] Villehardouin, *Memoirs or Chronicle of the Fourth Crusade and the Conquest of Constantinople.*

The new emperor proclaimed his intention to embark on a crusade to the Holy Land as soon as the empire was pacified and secured. Although the previous emperor, Mourtzouphlos, had been captured and executed, establishing control over the rest of the Byzantine Empire proved to be a challenging task.

Emperor Baldwin I received a quarter of the entire imperial territory, while half of the remaining three-quarters went to the Venetians. The other half was to be divided among the knights as imperial fiefs. Boniface of Montferrat was the most powerful among the knights as the king of Thessalonica. The greatest beneficiaries of this campaign were the Venetians, whose power was now based on possessing the most important ports and islands. The Venetians completely dominated the maritime route from their city to Constantinople, controlling even the entrance to Constantinople. Within the city, they had three-eighths of the urban territory, including Hagia Sophia.[i] The Frankish provincial princes had to swear an oath to the emperor of Constantinople, although Dandolo was exempt from this vassal obligation. Beyond the straits lay the remnants of Byzantine rule in Trebizond, Nicaea, and Epirus.

The Latin Empire could not survive politically, financially, or culturally. It was divided among too many larger and smaller rulers. A fragmented and complicated feudal system developed on the ruins of the Byzantine Empire. The Byzantine population hardly tolerated the Latin occupying power, mainly due to the arrogance of the conquerors and religious differences. The subordination of the Eastern Church to Roman authority was formally achieved but forcibly, not in the manner the pope had hoped for in terms of a union. According to Pope Innocent's plan, Byzantium was not to be subdued by arms but subordinated to the Holy See through a church union so that they could participate together in the Crusade. Foreign rule only deepened internal disunity.[ii]

On April 14$^{th}$, 1205, exactly one year after the capture of Constantinople by the Fourth Crusade, Emperor Baldwin I was captured, and Louis of Blois was killed at the Battle of Adrianople. The Latin army was defeated by the forces of Tsar Kaloyan of Bulgaria, who had allied with local Byzantine insurgents opposing Latin rule. The battle was a devastating blow to the Latin Empire. Following this defeat, papal legate

---

[i] Nicolle and Hook, *The Fourth Crusade 1202-04*.
[ii] Bartlett, *The Making of Europe*.

Peter of Capua recognized that the Crusade's original goal of reclaiming the Holy Land had become unattainable. He formally absolved those fighting for the Latin cause in Greece of their crusading vows.

After 1205, disaster followed the Latin rule, including the death of Boniface of Montferrat in battle in 1207. His so-called Kingdom of Thessalonica was annexed by the Epirote Greeks in 1224. After the crisis of 1205-06, the Latin Empire was governed by a series of regents, minors, and guardians who held the imperial title: Henry of Flanders, Peter de Courtenay, Robert de Courtenay, Baldwin II, and John of Brienne.[i] Between 1204 and 1261, Constantinople ceased to be a center of bureaucracy and consumption. It no longer represented a functional capital except in name only.

## The Restoration

The fall of Constantinople in 1204 was a turning point in Byzantine history, but it was not its end. While many Byzantine feudal lords submitted to the conqueror, joining the system of the new rule, and the common people, although dissatisfied, remained in their homeland, some Byzantine nobles left the occupied lands and moved to those provinces that were still unoccupied. Relying on the local Greek population, these refugees established new states in which Byzantium continued to live. In Asia Minor, Theodore Laskaris, the son-in-law of Alexios III, founded the Empire of Nicaea, and in the Balkans, Michael Angelos, the cousin of Isaac II and Alexios III, founded the Despotate of Epirus. A little earlier, independently of the fall of Constantinople, the Empire of Trebizond had been established on the southeastern coast of the Black Sea. It was founded by the grandsons of Andronikos I Komnenos, Alexios and David, who called themselves the Great Komnenoi, a name retained by later emperors of Trebizond.[ii]

The ruler of each of these states declared himself the true Byzantine emperor. They fought among themselves and against the Latins for control of the former lands of the Byzantine Empire. Although Epirus was initially the strongest of the three Greek states, the Nicaeans managed to take Constantinople from the Latins.[iii]

---

[i] Pears, *The Fall of Constantinople, Being the Story of the Fourth Crusade*.
[ii] Ostrogorsky, *History of the Byzantine State*.
[iii] Ibid.

# Chapter 15: The Palaiologoi: The Last Stand

## Restoration of the Empire

After the death of Emperor Theodore II Doukas Laskaris in 1258, his seven-year-old son, John IV, succeeded him. Due to the boy's age, Theodore appointed his trusted friend and court official, George Mouzalon, as regent. However, Mouzalon was assassinated shortly after Theodore's death—likely at the hands of aristocratic factions—and the regency passed to Michael Palaiologos, a powerful noble and military commander. Michael was soon proclaimed co-emperor and took control of the government.

During this period of political transition, neighboring powers took advantage of the weakened Byzantine position. While the Nicaean Empire remained intact, the earlier fragmentation of Byzantine authority had allowed both Bulgaria and Serbia to expand their influence. Although Bulgaria never fully regained its former golden age under Boris I and Simeon, it maintained a stable and sizable state. Serbia, under the rising Nemanjić dynasty, grew increasingly powerful and would pose a major threat to the Byzantine heartland in the 14th century.

The Latin Empire in Constantinople persisted for nearly sixty years following the Fourth Crusade. However, in 1261, General Alexios Strategopoulos exploited the absence of the Latin garrison and entered the city with a small force, reclaiming Constantinople for the Byzantines. This marked the restoration of the Byzantine Empire under Michael VIII Palaiologos, but it also ushered in a final phase of slow decline from which Byzantium would never fully recover.[i]

Latin influence would never recover again. After the capture of the capital, Michael ordered the blinding of John IV in order to become the supreme emperor. Patriarch Arsenios excommunicated Michael for this, but Arsenios was soon deposed and replaced by Joseph I. With Joseph's support, Michael began restoring monasteries and various public buildings. Hagia Sophia was renovated, and the harbor and walls of the city were fortified. Several hospitals, markets, and public baths were constructed, and a new mosque was built to replace the one destroyed during the Fourth Crusade. Byzantine rule was once again established in its glorious capital.

Michael VIII made significant contributions to the intellectual and cultural life of Byzantium. He initiated a dynasty that supported scholars, artists, and theologians, leading to the restoration of Constantinople as a center of learning and artistic production. Beginning in 1272, he formally co-ruled with his son, Andronikos II. This joint rule lasted for ten years and was characterized by the controversial union with the papacy in 1274 after the Second Council of Lyon.

After the death of Michael in 1282, Andronikos faced economic difficulties and internal strife, including conflicts with the aristocracy and the Orthodox Church. The threat of attack from the rising Turks became a reality, resulting in the loss of significant territories in Asia Minor. Despite appearances, Andronikos was not a weak ruler, and the circumstances he was involved in couldn't suppress his interest in science and literacy.[ii] Just as he co-ruled with his father, his son Michael IX assisted him. The concept of having two leaders is a notable characteristic of the Palaiologos dynasty. However, the practice of dividing the states among family members sparked disputes and led to internal strife.

---

[i] After being imprisoned by Theodore II, Alexios sided with Michael and quickly rose to the rank of grand domestic (*megas domestikos*), or commander-in-chief. He was directly below the emperor.

[ii] Ostrogorsky, George, *History of the Byzantine State,* Rutgers University Press, 1969, p. 447.

## Other Threats

Having faced continuous threats from the Latin states in Greece, the Ottoman Turks, and the Bulgarians and Serbs made Byzantines look for allies. Western European states provided alliances, but they were not always effective and often fragile.

The threat of invasion from the Turks in the east was not the main concern for Byzantium at that moment. The Serbian kingdom was gaining territories in the south, which was a major concern since the time of Serbian Grand Prince Stefan Nemanja (r. 1166-1196), reaching its peak during the reign of King Milutin II (r. 1282-1321). In 1282, Milutin captured Skopje, demonstrating his strength to the fallen Byzantium. Andronikos proposed to Milutin a marriage to his sister, Eudokia, but she stubbornly declined. To settle the situation and fearing Milutin's backlash, the Byzantine government proposed a marriage with Andronikos's five-year-old daughter, Simonida.[1] After their marriage in 1299, Byzantine influence rapidly grew in Serbia, although there would be numerous conflicts in the years to come.

Andronikos II lost his authority as he reached old age. Having less and less power, he became embroiled in a fight with his grandson Andronikos III, widening the gap between rivals. Various conflicts during Andronikos II's last three years of life in the First Palaiologan Civil War forced his inevitable abdication. Andronikos III attempted administrative and military reforms to strengthen the empire but faced internal opposition and losses to the Turks.

Despite the Byzantine Empire's decline, a new generation of aristocrats emerged, most notably John Kantakouzenos. As Serbia grew into a significant threat, Byzantium attempted to form an alliance with Bulgaria. However, the Serbian victory at the Battle of Velbazhd in 1330, where Tsar Michael Shishman was killed, thwarted these plans. The defeat weakened Bulgarian-Byzantine cooperation and marked the beginning of Serbian dominance in the central Balkans.

In the wake of this battle, political upheaval followed in both Bulgaria and Serbia. Ivan Alexander seized the Bulgarian throne, and Serbian nobles overthrew Stefan Uroš III and installed his son, Stefan Dušan. The alliance between these new rulers emboldened Dušan to campaign against

---

[1] Laskaris, Mihailo, *Vizantijske princeze*, Pešić i sinovi, 1997, p. 58.

Byzantium. Ongoing disputes among the Palaiologoi further undermined the empire, allowing Dušan to conquer much of Macedonia. Meanwhile, Andronikos III suffered defeats in Asia Minor at the hands of the Turks. Though he maintained relative control during his reign, his death in 1341 triggered a devastating civil war from which the Byzantine Empire never recovered.

## Civil Wars

When Emperor Andronikos III died in 1341, his nine-year-old son, John V Palaiologos, was named his successor. John VI Kantakouzenos, a powerful noble and former grand domestic, was expected to serve as regent. Kantakouzenos envisioned a revival of Byzantine strength. However, opposition quickly formed around the queen mother, Anna of Savoy, and Patriarch John XIV Kalekas, creating a hostile political environment. Quarrels and mistrust escalated into a civil war, plunging the empire into further instability. During this time, the Ottomans gained a foothold in the Balkans, Serbian forces under Stefan Dušan advanced toward Thessalonica, and the Bulgarians posed an ongoing threat.

John VI Kantakouzenos presiding over a synod.[48]

During such a vulnerable time, the opportunity for the opposition to rise couldn't go unnoticed. Patriarch John took over as regent, and Kantakouzenos was proclaimed an enemy. Alexios Apokaukos became the chief minister and head of the navy, making him one of the most powerful men in the Byzantine Empire.

This event led to a major crisis in Byzantium. There was a year-long war between Alexios's supporters and aristocrats loyal to Kantakouzenos, resulting in the decrease of power of the nobles. Seeing an opportunity to intervene, Serbian King Dušan welcomed Kantakouzenos in 1342 and formed an alliance with him. Despite initial setbacks, Kantakouzenos eventually declared himself emperor in Thessaly with the help of John Angel, the despot of Thessaly.

This surprising "selfish" ascension of his ally prompted Dušan to move toward Constantinople. The Palaiologos family, who had previously tried to gain Dušan's trust, now had the chance to bring him over to their side, especially since Dušan's son, Uros V, was married to John Palaiologos's sister.

Alexios Apokaukos, a bitter enemy of John VI Kantakouzenos, remained influential during the civil war and continued to wield harsh administrative control. By the end of his life, he had clamped down on political opponents, ordering executions and building a prison for his enemies. In 1345, during a visit to this newly constructed prison, Apokaukos was unexpectedly lynched by the inmates. With his chief rival gone and the Palaiologos faction significantly weakened, Kantakouzenos, who was supported by Ottoman forces, entered Constantinople and was crowned emperor.

However, the main beneficiary of the Byzantine turmoil was Stefan Dušan of Serbia. He had already captured Macedonia and Thessalonica and, in 1346, took Serres, declaring himself emperor of the Serbs and Greeks. After the civil war, he further expanded his empire, incorporating Thessaly and Epirus. His realm stretched from the Danube to the Gulf of Corinth and from the Adriatic to the Aegean Sea, absorbing many former Byzantine territories.

By this time, the Byzantine Empire had been reduced to a shadow of its former self, holding only parts of Thrace and a few scattered islands. Internal fragmentation, exacerbated by the distribution of provinces among various members of the Palaiologos family, further contributed to the collapse of centralized authority. A plague emerged in 1348 and continued to spread all over Europe for years.

The empire was in an abysmal state, and Dušan could have swooped in to end it all, but he suddenly died in 1355. His son Uros wasn't fit to keep his father's weakly solidified empire together. Byzantium was in such a poor state that it couldn't even bother to retrieve some of the territories Dušan had taken.

## The Battle of Kosovo

The rapid decline of Serbian power encouraged the Turks to occupy the Balkans. With no real power to fight back, the Turkish occupation of the Balkans reached its peak during the time of Sultan Murad I. The Serbian Empire was divided into many states, with the despotates of the nobles Ugljesa and Vukasin being the first in line to defend the Serbian Empire. The Battle of Maritza in 1371 saw both despots fall.

Andronikos IV conspired with others to start an uprising against his father, John V, but was stopped by Murad I. Andronikos was replaced by his brother Manuel II as co-emperor. Andronikos managed to escape imprisonment and, with the help of the Genoese, besieged Constantinople and breached the city. Alliances with the Ottomans helped them retake the Peloponnese from Kantakouzenos. Only the Serbs were able to offer some opposition to the impending Turkish occupation. The most powerful of the nobles, Prince Lazar, and his ally, King Tvrtko I, made an alliance with Byzantium.

The fateful battle took place on June 15$^{th}$, 1389, in Kosovo. The forces of Prince Lazar and his allies stood in front of Sultan Murad's army. The battle ended in a stalemate, although both leaders were killed during the fighting. Despite the indecisive outcome, the battle is significant for its impact on Serbian identity and for marking the beginning of Ottoman dominance. This became a symbol of Serbian resistance and delayed a larger Ottoman campaign.

After a hard-fought battle at Kosovo, the Ottoman heir, Bayezid I, continued to attack Byzantine lands. He used John VII, son of Andronikos IV, to retake Constantinople. After John V's death, both Manuel II and his nephew John VII sought an alliance with various European leaders. Backed by some and opposed by others, they were intermittently on the throne.

## Mongol Invasion and the Reduction of Ottoman Power

An even greater threat for the Turks, and subsequently everyone in the Balkans, came from the Far East: the Mongols, led by Timur. He founded the Timurid Empire in Persia and central Asia, claiming descent from Genghis Khan and seeking to restore the Mongol Empire. Timur's campaigns across central Asia, the Caucasus region, and parts of the Middle East were notorious for their brutality and massacres of civilians. Parts of Baghdad and Delhi were devastated to the point that they suffered a decline in urban life and economic activity for decades.

The Battle of Delhi in 1398, where Timur defeated Sultan Mahmud Tughlaq, was particularly brutal. After the passage of his hordes, "there couldn't be heard a dog barking ... or a kid crying."[i]

In 1402, Timur and Bayezid I clashed at the Battle of Ankara in central Anatolia. Although Bayezid had numerical superiority, Timur's tactical mastery—especially feigned retreats and encirclements—led to a decisive Ottoman defeat. Bayezid was captured, and the humiliation of the loss halted the Ottoman advance, triggering a decade-long civil war known as the Ottoman Interregnum.

Bayezid's defeat was later dramatized in European art, where he was often portrayed in an iron cage. However, contemporary sources suggest he was treated with relative respect. Timur died in 1405 while preparing to invade China. Despite his impressive conquests, his empire disintegrated shortly after his death and never rivaled the legacy of Genghis Khan.

The Ottoman Interregnum saw Bayezid's sons vying for control, a consequence of the harem-based succession system that bred internal rivalries. Ultimately, Mehmed I emerged victorious and reestablished unity by 1413, passing power smoothly to his son, Murad II. Despite an unsuccessful siege of Constantinople in 1422, the Ottomans gradually regained strength.

In the early 15th century, regional Christian leaders, including John Hunyadi of Hungary, Djuradj Branković of Serbia, and Skanderbeg of Albania, successfully resisted Ottoman incursions. While not connected to the Byzantine aristocracy, their efforts occasionally aligned with Byzantine interests and offered brief relief from Turkish pressure.

---

[i] Doukas 109, 20

## The Council of Florence

In 1439, the Council of Florence was held. Emperor John VIII sought to reunite the Eastern and Western Churches in hopes of securing military aid against the Turks. Although a formal union was declared, it was widely rejected in the Byzantine world and failed to deliver meaningful Western support.

The rule of the Palaiologos dynasty during the late Byzantine period was marked by a controversial attempt to unite the churches during the 1430s and 1440s. A formal agreement was signed by representatives of both churches in 1439. Pope Eugene IV convened the Council of Florence, where intense theological discussions and negotiations took place. A papal bull called *Laetentur Caeli* was issued, proclaiming the union of the churches. This temporary union aimed to gain Western support against the Ottomans but was deeply unpopular among the Byzantine clergy and aristocrats.

Despite occasional successes, the Byzantine emperor failed to stop the inevitable Ottoman expansion. The failed union deepened the schism and highlighted the complexities of theological differences and cultural divisions that shaped relations between the East and the West. As the union proved unstable and most likely to fail, the pope began planning a crusade against the Ottomans.

## The Battle of Varna

In 1444, a Christian alliance clashed with the Ottoman Turks near Varna on the Black Sea coast of present-day Bulgaria, where they suffered a significant defeat. The Christian coalition included Hungarian and Polish forces, with limited support from Wallachia, and was led by King Władysław III of Poland and Hungary. Military command was largely in the hands of John Hunyadi, a prominent Hungarian noble and general. This campaign was among the last major crusading efforts organized by Christian Europe with the intent of halting the advance of the Ottoman Empire and relieving pressure on Constantinople.

The alliance aimed to capitalize on internal instability within the Ottoman realm following Sultan Murad II's temporary abdication in favor of his son, Mehmed II. However, Murad returned to lead the Ottoman army in person. The arrival of a substantial Ottoman force near Lake Varna caught the Christian forces off guard, leading to internal disagreement over whether to retreat or attack. Ultimately, the decision was made to engage.

The battle initially favored the Christians, who managed to repel Ottoman attacks and pursued the retreating forces. However, the pursuit led to a breakdown in cohesion, and the Ottomans regrouped and counterattacked. In a decisive and ill-fated move, King Władysław led a charge with his personal guard against the Ottoman center in an attempt to break through to Murad's position. The charge failed, and Władysław was killed. His head was reportedly severed during the melee. His death triggered panic and a general rout among the Christian troops, leading to a devastating defeat.

The Battle of Varna marked a turning point in the struggle between Christian Europe and the expanding Ottoman Empire. It reinforced Ottoman dominance in the Balkans and underscored the declining capacity of European powers to coordinate effective military resistance during this period.

## The Fall of Constantinople

In 1449, Constantine XI Palaiologos was crowned emperor of Byzantium, succeeding his brother John VIII. By this point, the empire had been reduced to Constantinople and a few outposts, so it was highly vulnerable. Constantine sought assistance from Western powers, particularly after the death of Ottoman Sultan Murad II and the accession of his son, Mehmed II, in 1451.

Mehmed II, later known as "the Conqueror," was determined to capture Constantinople and end the Byzantine Empire. He assembled a large, diverse army and initiated extensive preparations for siege warfare. Among the most significant strategic moves was the construction of Rumeli Hisarı, a fortress on the European side of the Bosphorus, directly opposite the earlier Anadolu Hisarı. This allowed the Ottomans to control naval traffic and block aid from reaching the city by sea.

Despite efforts at an ecclesiastical union between the Eastern Orthodox and Roman Catholic Churches, Western aid was minimal. Some reinforcements arrived, such as a Genoese contingent under Giovanni Giustiniani and a small group of Neapolitan troops, but no substantial military support came in time. Venice, while sympathetic, reacted too slowly.

As part of the city's defense, the Byzantines placed a massive chain across the entrance to the Golden Horn, a narrow inlet forming Constantinople's northern harbor. However, in a bold maneuver,

Mehmed ordered Ottoman ships to be transported overland on greased logs to bypass the chain, allowing entry into the Golden Horn.

The defending force numbered around seven thousand men, including foreigners. The city's population had dwindled to roughly fifty thousand, while the Ottoman army is estimated to have numbered between fifty thousand and eighty thousand. They were equipped with siege cannons, including the massive Basilic cannon, which was capable of firing giant stone projectiles.

The Ottomans also attempted to undermine the city's fortifications by digging tunnels, some of which were discovered and destroyed by the defenders. On May 21$^{st}$, Mehmed offered terms of surrender to Constantinople, promising safe passage and preservation of property, but Emperor Constantine refused.

The final assault began after an extensive bombardment, which severely weakened the Theodosian Walls. On the morning of May 29$^{th}$, 1453, Ottoman forces breached the city. Emperor Constantine XI is believed to have died fighting on the front lines. The city was subjected to looting in accordance with the Ottoman custom of granting soldiers limited plunder after a successful siege.

Mehmed II's conquest of Constantinople earned him the title Fatih ("the Conqueror"), and he

Mehmed II entering the city of Constantinople."

subsequently transformed the city into the capital of the Ottoman Empire. This marked the end of the Byzantine Empire and a turning point in world history.

Hagia Sophia was converted into a mosque, marking the end of the Byzantine Empire and the medieval period in Europe. The Ottoman threat spurred European powers to explore trade routes and contributed to the Age of Exploration.

**The Successor States**

After the fall of Constantinople in 1453, the Despotate of the Morea in the southern Peloponnese remained one of the last remnants of the Byzantine world. Its capital, Mystras, had long been a flourishing center of Byzantine culture, attracting scholars, artists, and theologians during the empire's final centuries. The despotate was ruled by Constantine XI's brothers, Thomas and Demetrios Palaiologos, who had governed the region since the 1440s.

Following Constantinople's fall, the Morea became a target of Ottoman expansion. Internal strife between Thomas and Demetrios weakened the region further. In 1460, Ottoman forces under Sultan Mehmed II conquered the despotate. Some local nobles surrendered and were integrated into the Ottoman system, while others fled to western Europe, particularly Italy.

Athens fell to the Ottomans in 1458. The Parthenon, which had served as a Christian church dedicated to the Virgin Mary since the $6^{th}$ century, was converted into a mosque.

The other successor state was the Empire of Trebizond, located in northeastern Anatolia, with its capital at Trabzon. It was founded back in 1204 by Alexios I Komnenos following the Fourth Crusade. It flourished as a center of commerce and established relations with Georgia, uniting against the Ottomans. However, it ultimately fell under Ottoman rule in 1461, suffering a defeat from Mehmed II. The Ottoman Empire's superior forces forced the man in charge, David Komnenos, to surrender, ending the Empire of Trebizond. The nobles fled to Russia or Georgia.

# Bonus Chapter: Byzantine Art, Architecture, and Society

The Byzantine culture blended a variety of influences. Founded on the vestiges of the ancient Roman Empire, the Byzantine Empire was also impacted by a variety of Eastern influences, which can be seen in the art, architecture, and society of the Byzantine Empire.

This was visible from the very early days of the Byzantine Empire. Hagia Sophia, for instance, uses arches and domes, a skill mastered by ancient Romans (one only has to see the Pantheon to know this), but it also introduces elements not familiar to ancient Romans, such as new ways to stylize columns and capitals.

The Byzantines also stopped fluting their columns, which gave classical columns their characteristic look, with long grooves running along the surface. The Byzantines were much freer in this respect, producing a whole variety of columns and capitals. This is visible in the many columns of Hagia Sophia. This church has become a model for many Byzantine churches and churches in other Orthodox Christian countries. The Church of Saint Sava in Belgrade, Saint Alexander Nevsky Cathedral in Sofia, and the Cathedral of Christ the Saviour in Moscow, to mention only a few of the grandest structures, still stand as evidence of the far-reaching influence of the Byzantine Empire.

Capital from Hagia Sophia.[45]

Due to the sheer extent of the Byzantine Empire, we have many examples of Byzantine architecture all across Europe. In Ravenna, Italy, the Basilica di Sant'Apollinare Nuovo still stands as a testament to Byzantine influence. This basilica was rebuilt by Justinian I, and it features beautiful gold mosaics depicting Jesus and the most important moments in his life.

The Byzantines took the art of mosaic from the Greeks and Romans and brought it to another level (see the Komnenos mosaic, the Empress Zoë mosaic, and, the most impressive of all, the Deesis mosaic, all of which are in the Hagia Sophia). These large churches needed a lot of decoration, so more and more lavish and impressive mosaics were commissioned. Although the empire saw iconoclastic conflicts, visual art in the Byzantine Empire thrived in the form of mosaics and frescoes, which were regularly used to adorn the interiors of the many churches the empire erected.

A photo of Hagia Sophia from the late 19th century. The four minarets that surround the church were added later by the Ottomans.⁴⁶

Jesus Christ Pantocrator, a mosaic in Hagia Sophia.⁴⁷

There are, of course, many other buildings worthy of mention. The Hippodrome of Constantinople, built by Constantine the Great, was immense and could hold up to 100,000 spectators. The building hosted numerous sculptures and works of art, as was the case with the Hippodrome in Rome. One notable artifact transferred to the Hippodrome of Constantinople was the Serpent Column, originally a dedication from the Greek city-states to the sanctuary at Delphi, commemorating their victory over the Persians at the Battle of Plataea. It was moved to Constantinople by Emperor Constantine I as part of his efforts to adorn the new imperial capital with prestigious relics of the classical world.

Conversely, some treasures were later removed from Constantinople, particularly during the Fourth Crusade in 1204, when Latin Crusaders looted the city. Among the most famous were the gilded bronze horses that once adorned the Hippodrome. These sculptures were taken to Venice and installed atop the façade of St. Mark's Basilica, where they became known as the Horses of Saint Mark.

An important influence on Byzantine culture was, needless to say, Christianity. Because of the church, a lot of individuals were able to access contemporary and classical knowledge, and a lot of church officials, monks, and priests went on to make high-quality historical, philosophical, and poetic works. Theodoret of Cyrus was an early Byzantine author remembered for his hagiographical work. He wrote down and commented on the lives of the most important ascetics who lived in the Middle East during this period. We also have the Cappadocian Fathers—Basil the Great, Gregory of Nyssa, and Gregory of Nazianzus—known for their work on the concept of the Holy Trinity, which is in use to this day by all Christian churches.

However, there were other, somewhat more secular minds, such as Theodore Metochites, who wrote poetic works, and the more classical-oriented thinkers, such as Michael Psellos and especially his pupil, John Italus, who was accused of heresy for reintroducing ancient ideas like metempsychosis (the migration of souls).

Byzantine intellectuals played a major role in the Renaissance and the rediscovery of ancient works. With the gradual dissolution of the Byzantine Empire, Byzantine intellectuals, who were well versed in classical literature, migrated to Italy, where they participated in the revival of classical ideas.

## Byzantine Society

Byzantine society was very diverse, encompassing a wide range of ethnic, linguistic, and religious communities. The empire exerted significant and lasting cultural, political, and religious influence across several regions, including the Greek mainland, the broader Balkan Peninsula, the Middle East (notably Anatolia and parts of modern-day Syria), Egypt, and southern Italy.

The Byzantine society revolved around the imperial family and a number of wealthy, aristocratic families that vied for power. The power of these families came largely from the vast lands they owned, often for centuries. The lower classes were, themselves, a very diverse bunch. There were many highly educated and skilled workers, such as lawyers, clerks, teachers, bankers, and merchants, who sometimes could get very rich, although this did not automatically promote them to the aristocracy. The aristocracy was firmly entrenched in the bloodline, as well as land inheritance. What allowed skilled workers to move up a notch was their education, and education allowed at least some sort of class mobility in Byzantium, much as it does today.

Although craftsmen played a crucial economic role in Byzantine society—producing goods, supporting trade, and sustaining urban life—they were often regarded with a degree of condescension by the educated elite and aristocracy. This reflected the classical Greco-Roman ideal that manual labor, even when skilled, was inferior to intellectual or landowning pursuits. Social mobility decreased significantly in the lower tiers of society, with artisans and laborers typically having limited opportunities to rise in status. Craftsmen would usually pass their craft to their children, who were supposed to do the same job as their parents.

Then, there were free farmers who worked their own land, just enough to sustain themselves, and free farmers who owned no land and had to work other people's land in order to earn a living. The farmers' class was by far the most numerous (around 90 percent of the whole population).[i] Lastly were the slaves, who were below even the landless farmers. Slaves were bought and sold in the Byzantine Empire and procured through numerous conquests.

---

[i] Haldon, John F. The Byzantine Empire. The Dynamics of ancient empires: state power from Assyria to Byzantium, 2009, 205-254.

Although the Byzantine Empire is often mentioned as the first medieval state, slavery continued to be practiced.[i] In ancient Greece and Rome, the prevailing ideology condoned and justified the institution of slavery. The Christianity of the Byzantine Empire was, by definition, against slavery. However, the Byzantine Church managed to condone slavery.

Eunuchs were a very interesting subclass of the Byzantine Empire. They were employed in the royal palace as well as in state administration. The logic was the following: eunuchs were castrated, so they had no heirs and should have had no interest in organizing coups and assassinating emperors. Many slaves became state or aristocracy-owned eunuchs, and they were charged with a variety of jobs, such as serving and preparing food, keeping an eye on children, and doing household chores. The eunuchs could sometimes get very powerful, becoming generals or the emperor's personal advisors.

Byzantine society was deeply religious. The emperors were believed to be invested by God to rule. Natural catastrophes were interpreted as a sign from God that something was wrong with the state, and bold, successful usurpers were often seen as chosen by God to take the throne.

### Administration

While the emperor stood at the apex of Byzantine society, effective governance required a complex administrative system. Assisting him were members of the imperial household, including his wife, close relatives, and influential court eunuchs. In the earlier centuries of the empire, especially during the transition from Roman to Byzantine rule, praetorian prefects played a central role in managing vast regions of the empire.

During the late Roman period, the empire was divided into four major praetorian prefectures: the East (Orientis), Illyricum, Italy, and Gaul. Each was overseen by a praetorian prefect who managed taxation, justice, and administration. However, by Justinian's reign in the $6^{th}$ century, this system had begun to evolve. As Justinian reconquered lost western territories, he instituted new administrative structures, including the exarchates in Ravenna (Italy) and later Carthage (Africa), which combined civil and military authority in one office to better manage distant provinces.

---

[i] Slavery continued to be a thing in most medieval states, although it was less prominent in comparison to ancient times.

Below the prefecture level were dioceses. Usually, a prefecture consisted of several dioceses. A diocese, in turn, was divided into provinces, and a province was divided into poleis (cities) and their surrounding territories. Early on, the most important landlords in the cities were tasked with levying taxes, but as time moved on, the government was more in control of the tax system.

Let us briefly outline some of the most important titles in the Byzantine imperial hierarchy:

1. **Basileus (βασιλεύς)** - The official Greek title for the emperor, often paired with *autokratōr* (autocrat) to emphasize sole rule. The empress held significant ceremonial and sometimes political influence, often bearing titles such as Augusta or Autokratorissa. Imperial children born after their father's accession to the throne were called porphyrogenitus ("born in the purple"), referencing their birth in the Porphyra, a special chamber in the Great Palace decorated with purple stone.

2. **Despotes (δεσπότης)** - Literally meaning "lord," this was one of the highest court titles. It was often granted to the emperor's sons or sons-in-law. It signified a rank just below the emperor and was associated with ruling major provinces, such as the Despotate of the Morea, in later centuries.

3. **Sebastokrator (σεβαστοκράτωρ)** - A composite of *sebastos* ("venerable") and *kratōr* ("ruler"), this prestigious title ranked immediately after despotes and was typically given to close male relatives. It rarely applied to foreign rulers, who were more commonly styled as despotes.

4. **Kouropalates (κουροπαλάτης)** - Meaning "guardian of the palace," this title signified close proximity to the emperor and great courtly influence. Like many high court titles, it was often awarded to male relatives or distinguished allies. Also, certain palace roles—such as the *nipsistiarios*, a eunuch who assisted in imperial purification rituals—were of symbolic importance due to their ceremonial closeness to the emperor.

5. **Logothetes tou dromou (λογοθέτης τοῦ δρόμου)** - Head of the imperial postal and intelligence service, this official oversaw communication and foreign affairs. The office evolved from the *magister officiorum* of the late Roman bureaucracy and became one of the most powerful civilian roles in the empire.

6. **Military Titles** – The *megas domestikos* was the commander-in-chief of the Byzantine army, while the *megas doux* oversaw the imperial navy. Other notable ranks included the *stratopedarches*, a high-ranking general, and the *droungarios*, who commanded naval or cavalry units depending on the period. These roles formed the backbone of Byzantine military leadership, particularly in the empire's middle and late periods.

# Conclusion

The Byzantine Empire owed a lot to its geographical position between Europe and Asia. "New Rome" became the cradle of a new and powerful society. However, its precious position made the Byzantine Empire alluring to numerous invading forces. In the end, the Byzantine Empire was exposed to numerous attacks from all sides. Bulgarians, Slavs, Crusaders, and numerous Muslim invaders from Asia weakened the empire so much that the only thing that was left was the highly prized city of Constantinople, which finally succumbed to the unrelenting siege of the Ottoman Turks in 1453.

Nevertheless, Byzantine society continued to exist. The Byzantines were to submit to Ottoman rule, but their society was never completely destroyed. In fact, the hardships that the Ottomans brought to the Byzantines only served to strengthen the Byzantine-Greek identity, which finally broke out of subjugation in the $19^{th}$ century.

The Byzantine Empire is the second greatest Greek empire, coming centuries after the short-lived but illustrious Hellenistic empire of Alexander the Great. While Alexander's empire, in a way, lacked a decisive unifying factor, the Byzantine Empire found its unifying factor in the form of Christianity.

Crucially, the Byzantine Empire was able to spread its influence in Europe, shaping the cultures of countries such as Serbia, Bulgaria, North Macedonia, and Russia. Modern-day Greece, although proud of its ancient past, bears more evidence of the thousand years of the grand Byzantine Empire, which to this day fuels Greek national pride.

Today, there is a prospect of Greece having a conflict with Turkey, which continues to have a strong hold over Istanbul (or Constantinople as it was once called). Hagia Sophia functioned as a mosque for centuries and was made into a museum by the famous founder of the Turkish Republic, Ataturk. It has been recently converted back into a mosque, which was a symbolic act by the Turkish government that seeks to affirm its supremacy. Cyprus continues to be an island where Turkey and Greece quite literally clash. The animosity, rivalry, and conflict between the two countries spans around six hundred years. Will we see another European conflict, this time with the Greeks (possibly aided by a bigger power) facing the Turks?

It is important to note that the Byzantine Empire did not simply leave a sense of pride or a desire for revenge. It also brought cultural illumination to the Balkans and Russia. Millions and millions of Slavs today have to thank the Byzantine Empire since it brought not only religious and cultural influence but also very basic elements of society, such as the Cyrillic alphabet. Slavic peoples, such as Serbians, Russians, North Macedonians, and Bulgarians, in turn, continue to stay true to the Orthodox Christian faith of their ancestors. The influence of the Byzantine Empire is still very much felt today despite ceasing to exist around six hundred years ago.

Here's another book by Enthralling History that you might like

## Free limited time bonus

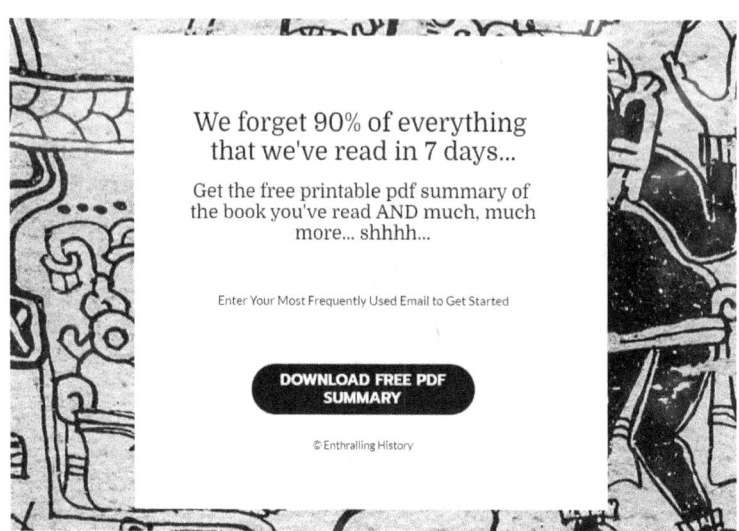

Stop for a moment. We have a free bonus set up for you. The problem is this: we forget 90% of everything that we read after 7 days. Crazy fact, right? Here's the solution: we've created a printable, 1-page pdf summary for this book that you're reading now. All you have to do to get your free pdf summary is to go to the following website: https://livetolearn.lpages.co/enthrallinghistory/

## Or, Scan the QR code!

Once you do, it will be intuitive. Enjoy, and thank you!

# References

"Emperor Constantine's Edict against the Arians." *fourthcentury.com*. 23 January 2010. Archived from the original on 19 August 2011. Retrieved 20 August 2011.

"Online Chapel - Greek Orthodox Archdiocese of America." *www.goarch.org*.

"The Antiquities of the Jews (13.298)." *Lexundria*.

Angold, Michael. *The Byzantine Empire, 1025-1204*.

Bartlett, Robert. *The Making of Europe*.

Besançon, Alain. *The Forbidden Image*.

Brubaker, Leslie, and John Haldon. *Byzantium in the Iconoclast Era (ca. 680-850)*.

Bury, J.B. *A History of the Later Roman Empire*.

Bury, J.B. *The Invasion of Europe by the Barbarians*. W.W. Norton & Company, 2000, p. 42.

Carlan, C.U. "Life and Death in the Ancient World: The Tetrarchy and the Last Persecution of Christians (303-311)."

Cleenewerck, Laurent. *His Broken Body*.

Diehl, Charles. *History of the Byzantine Empire*.

Dimitrov, Ivan Zhelev. "Bulgarian Christianity." In *The Blackwell Companion to Eastern Christianity*, 2007, p. 47.

Dunstan, W.E. *Rome*. Lanham, MD: Rowman & Littlefield Publishers, 2010. ISBN 9780742568341.

Edmondo, Lupieri. "Friar of Ignatius of Jesus (Carlo Leonelli) and the First 'Scholarly' Book on Mandaeaism (1652)." *ARAM Periodical* 16 (2004): 25-46.

Ehler, Sidney Zdeneck, and John B. Morrall. *Church and State Through the Centuries: A Collection of Historic Documents with Commentaries*. 1967.

Ehrman, Bart D. *Lost Christianities: The Battles for Scripture and the Faiths We Never Knew*. Oxford: Oxford University Press, 2005. pp. 95-112. ISBN 978-0-19-518249-1.

Fouracre, Paul, ed. *The New Cambridge Medieval History* Set.

Gonzalez, Justo. *The Story of Christianity*, Vol. 1. Harper Collins, 1984. p. 176. ISBN 0-06-063315-8.

Goodyear, Michael. "Compromised Defense – The Conquests of Basil II." *The Michigan Journal of History 5*.

Hamidovic, David. "About the Links Between the Dead Sea Scrolls and Mandaean Liturgy." *Aram Periodical* 22 (2010): 441-451.

Haldon, John. *Byzantium at War*.

Haldon, John F. "The Byzantine Empire." In *The Dynamics of Ancient Empires: State Power from Assyria to Byzantium*, 2009, pp. 205-254.

Handy, Lowell K. "The Appearance of Pantheon in Judah." In Diana Vikander Edelman (ed.), *The Triumph of Elohim: From Yahwism to Judaism*. Peeters Publishers, 1995.

Hitchcock, Susan Tyler, and John L. Esposito. *Geography of Religion: Where God Lives, Where Pilgrims Walk*. National Geographic Society, 2004. p. 281.

Holmes, Catherine. *Basil II and the Government of Empire (976-1025)*. PhD Thesis, University of Oxford, 1999.

Holmes, Catherine. "Basil II (AD 976-1025)." *De Imperatoribus Romanis*, 2003.

Holmes, Catherine. "Political Elites in the Reign of Basil II." In *Byzantium in the Year 1000*. Brill, 2003. pp. 35-69.

Houben, Hubert. *Roger II of Sicily*.

Howard-Johnston, James. *East Rome, Sasanian Persia and the End of Antiquity*.

Hunt, E.D. *Eusebius of Caesarea, Life of Constantine*. Translated by Averil Cameron and Stuart G. Hall. *The Journal of Ecclesiastical History* 52, no. 2 (2001): 338-396.

Hupchick, Dennis P. "Simeon's Campaigns for Imperial Recognition, 894-927." In *The Bulgarian-Byzantine Wars for Early Medieval Balkan Hegemony: Silver-Lined Skulls and Blinded Armies*, 2017, pp. 149-219.

Ilić, Nikola. "Da li je srpski knez Višeslav bio Hrišćanin?" *Teološki Pogledi* 55, no. 1: 95-112.

Jeffreys, Elizabeth. "The Beginning of Byzantine Chronography: John Malalas." In *Greek and Roman Historiography in Late Antiquity*. Brill, 2003. pp. 497-527.

Jedin, Hubert, John Dolan, and Karl Holland. *History of the Church.*

Kaldellis, Anthony. *Streams of Gold, Rivers of Blood.*

Kantakouzenos, John. *The History of John Kantakouzenos*, vol. II. Catholic University of America, 1979, p. 80.

Kennedy, Hugh. *The Great Arab Conquests.*

Kolrud, Kristine, and Marina Prusac. *Iconoclasm from Antiquity to Modernity.*

Krsmanović, Bojana, and Dejan Dželebdžić. "John Tzimiskes and Nikephoros II Phokas: The Background and Motives of a Premeditated Murder." *Zbornik radova Vizantološkog instituta* 47 (2010): 83–120.

Laskaris, Mihailo. *Vizantijske princeze.* Pešić i sinovi, 1997, p. 58.

Layton, Bentley. "Prolegomena to the Study of Ancient Gnosticism." In L. Michael White and O. Larry Yarbrough (eds.), *The Social World of the First Christians: Essays in Honor of Wayne A. Meeks.* Minneapolis: Fortress Press, 1995.

Leszka, Mirosław J. "The Monk versus the Philosopher: From the History of the Bulgarian-Byzantine War 894–896." *Studia Ceranea* 1 (2011): 55–70.

Liddell, Henry George, and Robert Scott. *A Greek-English Lexicon.* The Perseus Project.

Maier, Paul L. *Eusebius: The Church History.* Grand Rapids: Kregel Publications, 1999, p. 374.

Mashkin, Nikolai. *A History of Ancient Rome.* Gospolitizdat, 1956, p. 406.

Miller, Patrick D. *The Religion of Ancient Israel.* Westminster John Knox Press, 2000. ISBN 978-0-664-22145-4.

Mitchell, Stephen. *A History of the Later Roman Empire AD 284–641.* Oxford: Blackwell, 2007, p. 198.

Nicolle, David. *The Great Islamic Conquests, AD 632–750.*

Nicolle, David, and Christa Hook. *The Fourth Crusade 1202–04.*

Nestor. *Primary Chronicle*, p. 64. https://www.mgh-bibliothek.de/dokumente/a/a011458.pdf

Orlandis, José. *A Short History of the Catholic Church.*

Ostrogorsky, George. *History of the Byzantine State.* Rutgers University Press, 1969.

Pagels, Elaine. *The Gnostic Gospels.* New York: Knopf Doubleday, 1989. ISBN 978-0-679-72453-7.

Painter, Sidney. *A History of the Middle Ages 284–1500.* London: MacMillan Press, 1973, p. 33.

Pears, Edwin. *The Fall of Constantinople, Being the Story of the Fourth Crusade.*

Procopius. *The Secret History.* Penguin Books, 1982, p. 38.

Riley-Smith, Jonathan. *The Crusades.*

Richardson, Ernest C., Philip Schaff, and Henry Wace. *The Life of Constantine.* In *A Select Library of the Nicene and Post-Nicene Fathers of the Christian Church*, Series 2, 1890, vol. 2: 481-540.

Rukavishnikov, Alexandr. "Tale of Bygone Years: The Russian Primary Chronicle as a Family Chronicle." *Early Medieval Europe* 12, no. 1 (2003): 53-74.

Runciman, Steven. *Byzantine Civilization.*

Smith, M.D. "The Religion of Constantius I." *Greek, Roman, and Byzantine Studies* 38, no. 2 (1997): 187-208.

Socrates of Constantinople. *Church History*, Book 1, Chapter 33. In Anthony F. Beavers, *Chronology of the Arian Controversy.*

Sordi, Marta. *The Christians and the Roman Empire.* Norman: University of Oklahoma Press, 1994, p. 134.

Thaler, Kai. "Iraqi Minority Group Needs U.S. Attention." *Yale Daily News*, 9 March 2007. Retrieved 4 November 2021.

Theodoret of Cyrus. *The Ecclesiastical History of Theodoret*, Book 3, Chapter 31.

Villehardouin, Geoffrey. *Memoirs or Chronicle of the Fourth Crusade and the Conquest of Constantinople.*

Waldron, Byron Lloyd. *Diocletian, Hereditary Succession and the Tetrarchic Dynasty.* PhD diss., 2018.

Wheeler, Joe L. *Saint Nicholas.* Thomas Nelson, 2010.

Zosimus. *Historia Nova.* Translated by R.T. Ridley. *Zosimus: New History*, Byzantina Australiensia 2. Canberra, 1982.

# Image Sources

1 https://commons.wikimedia.org/w/index.php?curid=86235336
2 Capitoline Museums, CC BY-SA 3.0 <https://creativecommons.org/licenses/by-sa/3.0>, via Wikimedia Commons, https://commons.wikimedia.org/w/index.php?curid=25646964
3 Kunsthistorisches Museum, CC BY-SA 4.0 <https://creativecommons.org/licenses/by-sa/4.0>, via Wikimedia Commons, https://commons.wikimedia.org/w/index.php?curid=122518568)
4 Cplakidas, CC BY-SA 3.0 <https://creativecommons.org/licenses/by-sa/3.0>, via Wikimedia Commons, https://commons.wikimedia.org/w/index.php?curid=5084599)
5 https://commons.wikimedia.org/w/index.php?curid=117976
6 www.livius.org, CC BY-SA 4.0 <https://creativecommons.org/licenses/by-sa/4.0>, via Wikimedia Commons, https://commons.wikimedia.org/w/index.php?curid=92452046
7 User:MapMaster, CC BY-SA 2.5 <https://creativecommons.org/licenses/by-sa/2.5>, via Wikimedia Commons, https://commons.wikimedia.org/wiki/File:Invasions_of_the_Roman_Empire_1.png
8 https://commons.wikimedia.org/wiki/File:Sack_of_Rome_by_the_Visigoths_on_24_August_410_by_JN_Sylvestre_1890.jpg
9 No machine-readable author provided. Neuceu assumed (based on copyright claims)., CC BY-SA 2.5 <https://creativecommons.org/licenses/by-sa/2.5>, via Wikimedia Commons, https://commons.wikimedia.org/wiki/File:Justinien_527-565.svg
10 Petar Milošević, CC BY-SA 4.0 <https://creativecommons.org/licenses/by-sa/4.0>, via Wikimedia Commons,

https://commons.wikimedia.org/wiki/File:Mosaic_of_Justinianus_I_-_Basilica_San_Vitale_(Ravenna).jpg

11 Cplakidas, CC BY-SA 3.0 <http://creativecommons.org/licenses/by-sa/3.0/>, via Wikimedia Commons, https://commons.wikimedia.org/wiki/File:Constantinople_imperial_district.png)

12 Petar Milošević, CC BY-SA 4.0 <https://creativecommons.org/licenses/by-sa/4.0>, via Wikimedia Commons, https://commons.wikimedia.org/wiki/File:Empress_Theodora_mosaic_detail.png

13 Ghent University Library, CC BY-SA 4.0 <https://creativecommons.org/licenses/by-sa/4.0>, via Wikimedia Commons; https://commons.wikimedia.org/wiki/File:Archive-ugent-be-B96419FA-8AA4-11E3-9E68-C04DD43445F2_DS-441_(cropped).jpg

14 User Fphilibert from fr.wiki, CC BY-SA 3.0 <http://creativecommons.org/licenses/by-sa/3.0/>, via Wikimedia Commons, https://commons.wikimedia.org/w/index.php?curid=4577053)

15 Classical Numismatic Group, Inc. http://www.cngcoins.com, CC BY-SA 2.5 <https://creativecommons.org/licenses/by-sa/2.5>, via Wikimedia Commons, https://commons.wikimedia.org/w/index.php?curid=112987672)

16 Mohammad adil at the English-language Wikipedia, CC BY-SA 3.0 <http://creativecommons.org/licenses/by-sa/3.0/>, via Wikimedia Commons, https://commons.wikimedia.org/w/index.php?curid=5031572)

17 https://commons.wikimedia.org/w/index.php?curid=75718994

18 https://commons.wikimedia.org/w/index.php?curid=17019845

19 Ergovius, CC BY-SA 4.0 <https://creativecommons.org/licenses/by-sa/4.0>, via Wikimedia Commons, https://commons.wikimedia.org/wiki/File:Umayyad_Caliphate_720_AD_(orthographic_projection).svg

20 ByzantineEmpire717+extrainfo+themes.PNG: User:Amonixinatorderivative work: Hoodinski, CC BY-SA 3.0 <http://creativecommons.org/licenses/by-sa/3.0/>, via Wikimedia Commons, https://commons.wikimedia.org/w/index.php?curid=17633268)

21 https://commons.wikimedia.org/w/index.php?curid=3078150

22 https://commons.wikimedia.org/w/index.php?curid=114448071

23 https://commons.wikimedia.org/w/index.php?curid=4140266

24 https://commons.wikimedia.org/w/index.php?curid=42281965)

25 Own work, CC BY 4.0 <https://creativecommons.org/licenses/by/4.0>, via Wikimedia Commons, https://commons.wikimedia.org/w/index.php?curid=120098653

26 Ádám Kolláth, CC BY-SA 4.0 <https://creativecommons.org/licenses/by-sa/4.0>, via Wikimedia Commons, https://commons.wikimedia.org/w/index.php?curid=118846577)

27 https://commons.wikimedia.org/w/index.php?curid=2352102)

28 https://commons.wikimedia.org/w/index.php?curid=123642115

29 Wooofer, CC BY-SA 4.0 <https://creativecommons.org/licenses/by-sa/4.0>, via Wikimedia Commons, https://commons.wikimedia.org/w/index.php?curid=134238343

30 https://commons.wikimedia.org/w/index.php?curid=120420584

31 Unknown 10th-century artist, CC BY-SA 4.0 <https://creativecommons.org/licenses/by-sa/4.0>, via Wikimedia Commons, https://commons.wikimedia.org/w/index.php?curid=125448658

32 https://commons.wikimedia.org/w/index.php?curid=564187

33 https://commons.wikimedia.org/w/index.php?curid=11572784

34 Nécropotame (French version); Cplakidas (English translation), CC BY-SA 2.5 <https://creativecommons.org/licenses/by-sa/2.5>, via Wikimedia Commons, https://commons.wikimedia.org/w/index.php?curid=4078443

35 https://commons.wikimedia.org/w/index.php?curid=17017357

36 MapMaster, CC BY-SA 4.0 <https://creativecommons.org/licenses/by-sa/4.0>, via Wikimedia Commons, https://commons.wikimedia.org/w/index.php?curid=3692668

37 https://commons.wikimedia.org/w/index.php?curid=11349375

38 MapMaster, CC BY-SA 3.0 <http://creativecommons.org/licenses/by-sa/3.0/>, via Wikimedia Commons, https://commons.wikimedia.org/w/index.php?curid=1622291

39 https://commons.wikimedia.org/w/index.php?curid=23724829

40 https://commons.wikimedia.org/w/index.php?curid=5603413

41 https://commons.wikimedia.org/w/index.php?curid=111923528

42 https://commons.wikimedia.org/w/index.php?curid=3107592

43 https://commons.wikimedia.org/wiki/File:John_VI_Kantakouzenos.jpg

44 https://commons.wikimedia.org/wiki/File:Zonaro_GatesofConst.jpg

45 MM, CC BY-SA 4.0 <https://creativecommons.org/licenses/by-sa/4.0>, via Wikimedia Commons, https://commons.wikimedia.org/w/index.php?curid=45598631

46 https://commons.wikimedia.org/w/index.php?curid=11158906

47 Edal Anton Lefterov, CC BY-SA 3.0 <https://creativecommons.org/licenses/by-sa/3.0>, via Wikimedia Commons, https://commons.wikimedia.org/w/index.php?curid=15165689